# Plays for All Seasons

# Plays for All Seasons

*Drama through the Christian Year*

Derek Haylock

National Society/Church House Publishing
Church House, Great Smith Street, London SW1P 3NZ

National Society/Church House Publishing
Church House
Great Smith Street
London SW1P 3NZ

ISBN 0 7151 4884 2

Published in 1997 by The National Society and Church House Publishing

## Performing rights

## Photocopying

Cover design by Leigh Hurlock
Printed in England by The Cromwell Press Ltd, Melksham, Wiltshire.

# Contents

*Reprinted from *Acts for Apostles*, National Society/Church House
Publishing, 1987

# Introduction

I am often asked to provide some drama for schools, youth groups and churches, who want to put on something that will convey the particular aspect of the Christian message associated with various special days and seasons in the Christian calendar: Christmas, Easter, Harvest, and so on. *Plays for All Seasons* is a collection of scripted drama material written for just that purpose. In this collection I have tried to provide something for every likely occasion.

This book is the fifth in the series published by the National Society/Church House Publishing, following *Acts for Apostles* (1987), *Drama for Disciples* (1988), *Sketches from Scripture* (1992) and *Plays on the Word* (1993). Because there is a lot of interest in drama written for harvest thanksgiving services, but very little material available, we have decided to reprint here the two popular sketches on a harvest theme from Acts for Apostles. This is to ensure that these still-relevant and valued resources stay available when the earlier book is out of print.

As in the earlier books, this new collection uses a variety of styles, with plenty of humour and pace, where appropriate, but, I hope, sufficient seriousness and substance when dealing with important biblical truths. Most of the material is technically straightforward and can be put on with fairly minimal rehearsal. Some pieces are written to be performed by children or young people, others by adults. However, since many pieces I have written for adults have, to my surprise, been put on very successfully by children (and vice versa!), I have decided not to stipulate the intended age of the performers in this new collection.

Although each piece is linked here with a special time of the year, many of the sketches could be performed at other times than those indicated. For example, one church youth group is planning to use *I Wonder What Happened To Him* on Good Friday as well as at Christmas. One drama group is planning to put on the play written for Education Sunday (*Gardeners' Question Time*) at a Young Church Anniversary service. Some sketches, such as *Farmer Jack, The Rich Fool* and *Tug of War* could be used at any time of the year.

Quotations from the Bible are taken mainly from *The New International Version* (1978), published in Great Britain by Hodder & Stoughton.

It is my sincere prayer that these simple plays will be used to communicate the truth of the Word of God, in a lively, challenging and relevant fashion. All the material in this book has been tried and tested either by the adult drama group or the young people at my own church, Surrey Chapel in Norwich. I am particularly grateful to Gill Blake, Tony Blake, Rachel Girling and Amanda Johnson for their help in trying out and developing the final versions of many of the plays. It is always encouraging for me to hear how other groups and their audiences have responded to my material. So do let me know how you get on with *Plays for All Seasons*!

Derek Haylock

Postal address: EDU, UEA, Norwich NR4 7TJ

e-mail: d.haylock@uea.ac.uk

# Message received, but not understood

### (*Advent*)

## Introduction

This sketch is a modern-day parable about the coming of the promised Saviour and the way in which people failed to recognise him for who he was.

## Bible base

*John 1. 10–11; Philippians 2. 7–8*

## Cast

Seven actors, A, B, C, D, E, F, G, all dressed in factory-style clothes

*The scene is a factory. The precise nature of the factory output is never mentioned. A and B are on stage, standing stage left, looking into the distance, off-stage.*

A       So, you've seen it as well?

B       Yes. I was just surfing the Internet during my lunch break and there it was.

A       Do you believe it?

B       Not sure. You get all kinds of misleading info on the Net these days. But I'd like to believe it. It'd be just what the factory needs.

A       Yes. It would. We've plenty of problems that need sorting.

C       (*Entering and joining them*) What's going on? There's a buzz going round the factory.

B       Haven't you heard?

C       Heard what?

| | |
|---|---|
| A | We've picked up a rumour on the Net. |
| B | Electronic message. From the States. |
| A | If it's true, he could be arriving any time! |
| C | Who? Surely you don't mean . . . ? |
| B | Yes. The boss. |
| C | Wow! He's never come here before, has he? |
| A | Not since I started. |

(*D and E enter, excitedly, and join them.*)

| | |
|---|---|
| D | Any sign of him? |
| E | It's exciting, isn't it! |
| B | If it's true. |
| D | What time is he expected? |
| A | Any minute now. |
| B | But it's only a rumour. It may not be true. |
| F | (*Entering, but standing at the back away from the others*) What's going on? Why is everyone on edge? |

(*The others talk to F, but keep looking ahead of them into the distance.*)

| | |
|---|---|
| A | There's a rumour that the boss is coming. |
| B | Any time now. |
| F | The boss? |
| C | Yes, the boss. The owner. The chairman of the company. Himself. |
| D | Actually coming here! To his own factory! |
| F | So, why's everyone so excited? |
| E | (*Gesturing towards F*) Is he new here or something? |
| F | Well . . . (*looking at watch*) . . . I haven't been here long. |
| E | Well, the boss . . . he made this place. |
| A | They say he built it with his own hands. Brick by brick. |
| B | Breeze block by breeze block. |
| C | The whole concern was paid for out of his own pocket. |

**2**

| | |
|---|---|
| D | He built it up from nothing. |
| E | We owe everything to him. |
| A | Our jobs. |
| B | Our security. |
| C | Our lives. |
| F | Have any of you seen him before? |
| A | Course not. He's not been here for years. Not since any of us came. |
| F | So how will you recognise him when he comes? |
| B | Oh, it'll be obvious enough. |
| C | He must be very wealthy. You know, smart suit, silk tie. |
| D | Big flashy car. Roller, I should think. |
| E | Chauffeur-driven. |
| F | So, why's he coming? |
| A | If he's coming. It is only a rumour. |
| B | He'll be coming to sort out some of the problems. |
| F | Problems? |
| C | In the factory. Some of the disputes. |
| D | You know the kind of thing. Management and work-force. |
| E | Endless arguments. |
| A | Discrimination. |
| B | Exploitation. |
| C | Victimisation. |
| D | Poor working conditions. |
| E | Corrupt management. |
| F | What? Is all that going on here? |
| A | He obviously is new here. |
| F | So, when are you expecting him? |
| B | About five minutes ago. |

C     I don't think he's coming.

D     It was only a rumour.

E     You can't trust the stuff you read on the Internet.

A     I'm getting tired of waiting.

*(They gradually start to drift off and exit one by one.)*

B     I never believed it anyway.

C     I'm going back to work.

D     So am I.

E     Yes. That's it. Obviously not coming.

A     I'm off.

B     Me too.

*(F is now left on his own. He looks around. After a while G enters.)*

G     So, were they expecting you, boss?

F     Well, not really.

G     But I definitely put the message on the Net? Didn't they pick it up?

F     Message received, but not understood, I'm afraid. They seemed to be expecting . . . someone completely different.

G     So they didn't realise that you would be, well, just like one of them . . .

F     And that I had to be, if I was going to be on their side, sorting out the problems.

G     So, shall we try the next factory then, boss?

F     Looks like it.

*(They start to exit. Then F stops, looks around and stretches out his hands with palms turned upwards.)*

      I came to that which was my own, and they did not receive me. They didn't even recognise me.

G     Will it always be like this, boss?

F     Sometimes . . . Often . . . But, not always.

*(They exit.)*

**4**

# An orderly account

## (Bible Sunday)

### Introduction

Bible Sunday is an opportunity to give thanks that God reveals himself and his truth to us through his written Word. This sketch sets out to highlight one aspect of the New Testament writings about the life and work of Jesus: the historical reliability of the Gospels' account of the life of Christ, particularly the precise attention to detail in the account of Luke (see Luke 1. 1–4). This conversation between Luke and Peter is how we might imagine Luke the Gospel-writer set about getting absolutely right the details of the extraordinary catch of fish and Peter's call by Christ. The sketch could usefully be followed by a reading of Luke 5. 1–12, thus serving to draw the audience's attention to the extensive historical detail in Luke's recounting of the incident.

### Bible base
*Luke 1. 1–4 and 5. 1–12.*

### Cast
Luke

Peter

*There is a table centre stage and two chairs. On the table, there are paper and writing implements. Luke enters and addresses the audience . . .*

**Luke**    Many have undertaken to draw up an account of the things that have been fulfilled among us, just as they were handed down to us by those who from the first were eye-witnesses and servants of the word. But I, Luke, am investigating everything about Jesus, from the beginning. Then it will seem good to me to write an orderly account for you, so that you may know the certainty of the things you have been taught.

*(Peter enters.)*

Ah, Peter, there you are. Right, let's get to work.

*(They sit at the table. Luke makes careful notes throughout the conversation.)*

Now, Peter, let's just go over this again and make sure I've got it right. 'One day as Jesus was standing by a lake . . .' Which lake?

| | |
|---|---|
| Peter | Lake Gennesaret. That's the Sea of Galilee, as we call it. |
| Luke | Right. ' . . . by Lake Genessaret.' Is that one n and two s's? |
| Peter | Don't ask me, I'm . . . |
| Together | . . . just a humble fisherman. |
| Luke | Now help me get the picture absolutely right. Jesus preaching the word of God, right? |
| Peter | Right. By the edge of the lake. |
| Luke | And the people listening? |
| Peter | All crowding round him. |
| Luke | OK. People crowding round Jesus. So he looks round . . .? |
| Peter | . . . and sees the boats. |
| Luke | How many boats? |
| Peter | Two. |
| Luke | What were they doing there? |
| Peter | They were ours – me and my partners. We'd left them there while we were washing our nets. |
| Luke | OK, so Jesus got into one of the boats. Which one? |
| Peter | My one. |
| Luke | Right. ' . . . the one belonging to Peter.' |
| Peter | That should be Simon. I was still called Simon then. |
| Luke | Of course. So what happened next? |
| Peter | He asked me to put out from the shore. |
| Luke | A long way? A short distance? |

| | |
|---|---|
| Peter | Just a little distance from the shore. Then he started to teach the people, from the boat. |
| Luke | OK, got that. Um, standing up? Sitting down? |
| Peter | Oh, he sat down. Safer that way. (*Sarcastic*) In a boat. |
| Luke | All right, bear with me. I just want to get the details absolutely right. Remember I want to be able to tell them that I have carefully investigated everything about Jesus, from the beginning. |
| Peter | Yes, doctor. |
| Luke | Now. When he had finished speaking to the crowd, he spoke to you . . . . Exact words? |
| Peter | (*Remembering, slowly*) 'Put out into deep water, and let down the nets for a catch.' Yes, that was it. |
| Luke | And you replied? |
| Peter | Well, I told him we'd worked hard all night and hadn't caught anything. |
| Luke | ' . . . hadn't caught anything.' Exactly how would you have addressed him at that time? Lord? Sir? Rabbi? |
| Peter | Master, I suppose. And then I said, 'But because you say so, I will let down the nets.' |
| Luke | Great. Now you did this and what happened? |
| Peter | Well, we caught a lot of fish. |
| Luke | A lot? What's a lot? Fifty? A hundred? |
| Peter | Who knows! Such a large number the nets began to break! |
| Luke | So your partners came to help in the other boat. Was that their own idea? |
| Peter | No, we signalled to them. |
| Luke | And you filled both boats with fish? |
| Peter | That's right – so full they began to sink! |
| Luke | Now this bit about how you reacted. You fell to the ground in front of Jesus. At his feet? |

**7**

| | |
|---|---|
| Peter | More knees, actually. Yes, knees rather than feet. |
| Luke | You remember what you said? Precisely? |
| Peter | Precisely! I said to him, 'Go away from me, Lord . . .' |
| Luke | Lord? You called him Lord? You sure about that? |
| Peter | Oh yes! So I did. It just came out. 'Go away from me, Lord. I am a sinful man.' |
| Luke | So, here's the inevitable question. Tell me, Peter, how did you feel when you saw this catch of fish? |
| Peter | How did I feel? I was just astonished! Frightened almost, wondering who this was we were dealing with. And so were my partners. |
| Luke | ' . . . and so were Simon's partners.' Ah, we haven't given their names. That was James, and . . .? |
| Peter | James and John. They were brothers. |
| Luke | Oh, yes. 'James and John.' Father's name? |
| Peter | Oh yes, they were Zebedee's sons. |
| Luke | ' . . . the sons of Zebedee.' Now tell me again, this bit that Jesus said to you about catching men rather than fish. Make sure I've got the words right. |
| Peter | He said, 'Don't be afraid, Simon . . .' |
| Luke | 'Afraid?' Ah, yes, you're down there on your knees, trembling, aren't you! |
| Peter | 'Don't be afraid, Simon . . . from now on you will catch men.' |
| Luke | Got it. Good. And then you followed him. Right? |
| Peter | Right. |
| Luke | One more detail. The boats. Your nets? The fish! What's happened to them? |
| Peter | We just pulled the boats up on to the shore – and, well, we just left them all there and followed Jesus. |

**Luke**     ' . . . left everything and followed him.' Great. Thanks, Peter, you can get back to your church meeting now.

(*Peter gets up to leave.*)

Oh, and if Mary's there, could you ask her to come over when she has a moment and check the wording of the Magnificat with me?

# I wonder what happened to him

## (*Christmas*)

### Introduction

This is a sketch that explores the real meaning of the events of the first Christmas. It starts in a light-hearted fashion, with a string of pretty awful jokes, but then gradually moves to a more serious note pointing from Christmas to Good Friday.

### Bible base

*Luke 2. 1–20.*

### Cast

Three labourers, Ashbel, Ben and Caleb:
Ashbel is the boss and clearly in charge;
Ben is a bit of a joker;
Caleb is rather slow on the uptake.
Also required (but optional): a solo soprano to sing off-stage.

*The scene is Bethlehem, thirty-odd years after the birth of Christ. For the greatest effect at the end of the sketch there should be a light shining from behind the actors. The three labourers are dismantling the stable (which is presumed to be just off-stage, stage right). There should be a total blackout, during which a solo soprano voice sings the following verse (Tune:* Wondrous Story) *– if no singer is available this can easily be omitted both here and at the end.*

**Soprano** Who is he in yonder stall,

     at whose feet the shepherds fall?

     'tis the Lord, O wondrous story!

'tis the Lord, the King of glory.

At his feet we humbly fall,

crown him, crown him Lord of all.

(*The lights on stage come up. Ashbel is seated stage left on a low stool and is recording items in a book, as though keeping accounts. There is a box centre stage and another low stool stage right. Ben and Caleb are off-stage, stage right. The noise of them dismantling a building can be heard. There is a loud crash.*)

| | |
|---|---|
| **Ashbel** | (*Calling out*) Go easy on those beams! They're worth a few shekels. |
| **Ben** | (*Entering from off-stage, looking exhausted*) All right, all right. It's all very well for you, Ashbel, sitting there doing nothing while we do all the hard work. |
| **Ashbel** | I do the technical stuff, you two do the heavy labour. That's team-work. |
| **Ben** | (*Sitting down on the box and sharing a drink with Ashbel*) Phew! I need a break. And some fresh air. Cor, the smell in there. It's awful. |
| **Ashbel** | Used to be a stable, you know. Probably kept cows and donkeys in there. |
| **Ben** | (*Pointing off-stage*) Caleb used to keep a donkey in his front room. |
| **Ashbel** | Ugh! What about the smell? |
| **Ben** | After a couple of weeks the donkey got used to it! |
| **Caleb** | (*Popping head round the corner*) Someone mention my name? |
| **Ashbel** | No, we were talking about, um, that other guy, um, you know . . . old Caleb who came down from Galilee. Used to deal in second-hand camels. |
| **Ben** | That's right. Do you remember old Caleb? Had a stall just on the outskirts of town. |
| **Caleb** | (*Talking from the edge of the stage*) Oh, yeah. I wonder what happened to him . . . |

| | |
|---|---|
| **Ben** | The police found out he'd been fiddling the mileage on his camels and he had to leave Bethlehem in a hurry. Disappeared into the Negev desert a couple of years ago on a camel, with only half a tankful of fuel. Never seen again. |
| **Ashbel** | We've had some characters living in Bethlehem over the years, haven't we! Do you remember that old girl called . . . Annie, wasn't it? She used to go round cleaning out all the stables in Bethlehem? |
| **Ben** | Oh, yeah, Annie the peripatetic muck-scraper. |
| **Ashbel** | Now she really did smell! |

(*They all react appropriately, holding noses and so on.*)

| | |
|---|---|
| **Caleb** | I wonder what happened to her? |
| **Ashbel** | Never you mind, Caleb. You just get that stable cleared up. |
| **Caleb** | (*Sarcastically*) Yes, master. (*Goes back off-stage and calls out, while audibly moving stuff around*) Urgh! What shall I do with a pile of rotting straw? |
| **Ashbel** | Burn. |
| **Caleb** | Sacks? |
| **Ashbel** | Chuck. |
| **Caleb** | Broken manger? |
| **Ashbel** | Firewood. |
| **Caleb** | Rusty horse-shoe? |
| **Ashbel** | Recycle. |
| **Ben** | Come and have a break, Caleb. I'll give you a hand with the heavy stuff in a while. |
| **Caleb** | (*Entering and joining them for a drink*) Thanks, Ben. I never thought that dismantling an old stable would be such a job. There you are. One rusty horseshoe. For recycling. |
| | (*Drops an old horseshoe in front of Ashbel and sits down on the remaining stool*) |
| **Ashbel** | (*Picking up the horseshoe*) Do you remember old Ezad the iron-monger? |

**12**

**Caleb**   Oh, yeah. I wonder what happened to him?

**Ben**   He kicked the bucket.

*(Ben finds it difficult to hold back his laughter: this increases with the following jokes!)*

**Ashbel**   And then there was old Jonah the candle-maker.

**Caleb**   Oh, yeah. I wonder what happened to him?

**Ben**   He snuffed it . . . !

**Ashbel**   And what about that old woman, Miriam, who used to take in washing?

**Caleb**   Oh, yeah. I wonder what happened to her?

**Ben**   She pegged out . . . !

**Ashbel**   And that old chap who used to sell goose-grease . . .

**Caleb**   Jethro, wasn't it? I wonder what happened to him?

**Ben**   *(Pause)* He slipped away quietly in the night.

**Ashbel**   Ah, well, as the Romans say, sic transit gloria mundi . . .

**Caleb**   I wonder what happened to her?

*(Ashbel and Ben look puzzled.)*

Gloria Mundi . . .

*(Ashbel and Ben react appropriately, throw things at Caleb, etc!)*

**Ashbel**   This place used to belong to old Daniel and Esther, you know, the couple who ran the inn round the corner.

**Caleb**   Oh, yeah, I remember them. Went to school with old Dan. I wonder what happened to him . . .

**Ben**   I heard they made so much money during the census, they sold up and moved to a posh place in Jerusalem.

**Ashbel**   Cor, do you remember that census? Must have been . . . what? Thirty years ago now . . .

**Ben**   Never forget it.

**Caleb**   Never seen the town so crowded.

| | |
|---|---|
| **Ashbel** | Come to think of it, wasn't it . . . ? That's right. Here. In the stable . . . |
| **Caleb** | The stable? What was it? |
| **Ben** | It was a sort of shed in which animals were kept. |
| **Ashbel** | No, listen. Don't you remember. During the census. There was that young couple, came down from somewhere up north for the census. He was a carpenter. |
| **Ben** | Oh, yes . . ., J . . ., J . . ., Joshua? Jonah? No, Joseph, that was it. Joseph, the carpenter. |
| **Ashbel** | They were engaged to be married, but the girl, well, she was, you know, pregnant. Well, they finished up in there, in that stable. I'm sure it was. No room at old Dan's inn, so the girl had to have the baby in there. |
| **Caleb** | Oh yeah, I remember now. (*Pause*) I wonder what happened to them. |
| **Ben** | There was a bunch of shepherds running round the next day, telling everyone that a saviour had been born. In a stable! Huh! |
| **Ashbel** | A saviour! That's a joke. When we've still got the Romans running the country and making our lives a misery. |
| **Ben** | Come on, Caleb, let's get those beams down. |

(*Ben and Caleb exit.*)

| | |
|---|---|
| **Caleb** | You two make my life a misery. |
| **Ashbel** | (*Standing up and calling out*) At least we can sell them beams to the Romans. I'm sure they'll find a use for them . . . |
| **Caleb** | (*Entering, carrying a beam, about five foot in length*) I remember now. His name. Jesus, it was. The baby. Yes, that was his name. Jesus. Funny that. (*Thoughtfully*) It means saviour. |
| **Ben** | (*Calling from off-stage*) Come on, Caleb, give us a hand with this one. |
| **Caleb** | (*Poignantly, studying the beam closely*) He could probably have made good use of this wood, couldn't he . . . you know, if he went into his father's business. |
| **Ben** | Come on, Caleb . . . |

**14**

**Caleb**     (*To Ashbel*) Here, hold on to this a mo . . .

(*Caleb passes the beam to Ashbel, who stands just to the left of the box, with the beam over his left shoulder, looking away from the audience.*)

**Ashbel**     Come on, hurry up. This weighs a ton.

(*Caleb enters again, followed by Ben. Caleb is carrying another beam, about seven foot in length.*)

**Caleb**     That's right. Jesus. That was his name. Definite.

(*Caleb sits on the box, thoughtfully, holding the beam vertically, so that it is absolutely centre stage.*)

**Ben**     (*Sitting on the stool, stage right*) Some people said he was sent by God to save us from our sins.

**Ashbel**     (*Quite aggressively*) And how precisely would he do that, eh?

(*As he delivers this line Ashbel turns stage right to face Ben, so that the beam on his shoulder forms a cross with the vertical beam supported by Ashbel.*)

**Ben**     No idea.

(*All lights go down except the lights from the back of the stage, leaving the cross silhouetted against the light.*)

**Caleb**     Yes, that was his name. Jesus. I wonder what happened to him?

(*They freeze. The soprano voice off-stage then sings.*)

**Soprano**     Who is he on yonder tree,

gives his life for you and me?

'tis the Lord, O wondrous story!

'tis the Lord, the King of glory.

At his feet we humbly fall,

crown him, crown him Lord of all.

# We can't see Jesus!

## (Christmas)

## Introduction

This sketch sets out simply to make the point that all the trappings of contemporary Christmas actually make it difficult for people to see Jesus in it all.

## Bible base

*Luke 2. 1–20*

## Cast

Mary and Joseph
Inn-keeper
Two or three Shepherds (all these non-speaking parts)
Two Observers, A and B
Reader (off-stage)
The 'Obstructions':
Shopper
Christmas Tree
Christmas Card
Two Party-goers
Persons C and D
Father Christmas

*On one side of the stage there is a crib, in a traditional Christmas nativity-scene setting. The 'baby' should be already in the crib, but not visible. On the opposite side are two chairs on which are seated the two observers, A and B. The other participants (various 'obstructions') will assemble in the middle of the stage, gradually blocking the view of the two observers. The sketch begins with the two observers talking to each other.*

| | |
|---|---|
| A | Christmas again, then. |
| B | Yep. Lots to do. But I had to find time for this. |
| A | You here for the same reason as me? |
| B | What's that then? |
| A | To see the Christmas story again. You know, the nativity-whatsit. |
| B | Yes! We'll see it all right from here then? |
| A | Yes. Excellent view. |
| B | Ooh, I think it's just about to start. |
| A | Goodie. I'm really looking forward to seeing the baby Jesus and all that. |
| B | Ssh! It's starting. |
| Reader | (*Off-stage*) In those days Caesar Augustus issued a decree that a census should be taken of the entire world. |
| A | The entire world!? |
| B | Well, just the Roman Empire, actually. |
| A | Oh, I see. |
| Reader | And everyone went to his own town to register. |
| A | I suppose they didn't have first class postal services. |
| B | Or fax-machines. |
| A | Or E-mail. |
| B | Or mobile phones. |
| Reader | So Joseph also went up from the town of Nazareth in Galilee to Judea, to Bethlehem the town of David . . . |
| A | (*Pointing in the direction of the crib*) That'll be Bethlehem over there. |

(*Mary and Joseph enter, passing the two observers, as the reading continues, walking slowly towards the crib.*)

| | |
|---|---|
| Reader | . . . because he belonged to the house and line of David. |
| B | There's Joseph, on his way to Bethlehem. |

**17**

| | |
|---|---|
| **A** | And that'll be Mary with him. |
| **Reader** | He went there to register with Mary . . . |
| **A** | See, I was right. |
| **Reader** | . . . who was pledged to be married to him and was expecting a child. |
| **B** | Ah! She looks so young. |

(*The Inn-keeper enters from the other side and greets Mary and Joseph, shaking his head and pointing to the crib, as the reading continues, then exits. Mary and Joseph move to the crib.*)

| | |
|---|---|
| **Reader** | While they were there the time came for the baby to be born, and she gave birth to her first-born, a son. |
| **A & B** | (*Soppily*) Ahhh . . . |
| **Reader** | Because there was no room for them in the inn, she wrapped him in strips of cloth and laid him in a manger. |

(*Mary and Joseph sit down beside the crib. Mary attends to the baby.*)

| | |
|---|---|
| **A & B** | (*Sympathetically*) Ohhhh . . . |

(*A modern-day shopper, laden with carrier-bags, suddenly bursts in and takes up position centre stage, in a panic.*)

| | |
|---|---|
| **Shopper** | Christmas! Shopping, shopping, shopping! That's all it is. So much to buy. Turkey. Brussels sprouts. Christmas cake. Christmas pudding. Brandy sauce. Mince pies. Hot cross buns. Wrapping paper. Tinsel. Look at my list! (*Produces and unfolds a great long list*) |
| **A** | Excuse me! (*Trying to peer round the shopper at the crib*) |
| **Shopper** | Look at my list! (*Moving to one side and freezing*) |
| | Look at my list! |
| **B** | Thank you. Now can we carry on please? |
| **Reader** | And there were shepherds living out in the fields near by, keeping watch over their flock by night. |

(*Two or three shepherds enter and move to the centre of the stage.*)

| | |
|---|---|
| **A** | I like this bit. |

**18**

**Reader**   An angel of the Lord appeared to them . . .

*(The shepherds fall on their knees, looking upwards.)*

. . .and the glory of the Lord shone around them, and they were terrified. But the angel said to them, 'Do not be afraid . . .'

**A**   *(To the shepherds)* No, don't be afraid!

**B**   It's only an angel.

**Reader**   '. . . I bring you good tidings of great joy that will be for all the people.'

*(Suddenly, someone carrying a large Christmas tree in front of them comes marching in, and takes up position centre stage in front of the shepherds.)*

**Tree**   The Christmas tree.

*(Recites)*

A Christmas tree is just the thing

To bring you Christmas joy.

My branches carry little gifts

For every boy and girl . . . *(correction)* um . . . girl and boy.

*(Singing and doing a little dance)*

'O Christmas tree, O Christmas tree,

O tree of green, unchanging . . .'

**A**   Excuse me! *(Trying even harder to see the crib)*

*(The Tree dances around singing, 'O Christmas tree, O Christmas tree', while the Shopper leaps into life waving her list, shouting, 'Look at my list! Look at my list!')*

**A & B**   *(Both straining to see the crib)* Excuse me!

*(The Tree and the Shopper freeze.)*

**B**   Thank you! Now can we carry on please?

*(As the sketch continues A and B find it more and more difficult to see what is going on in Bethlehem.)*

**Reader**   'Today, in the town of David a Saviour has been born to you. He is Christ the Lord. This will be a sign to you: you will find a baby wrapped in strips of cloth and lying in a manger.'

**19**

| | |
|---|---|
| **B** | I was an angel once. |
| **A** | (*Incredulous*) What!? |
| **B** | In our school Christmas play. |
| **A** | Oh. |
| **Reader** | Suddenly, a great company of the heavenly host . . . |
| **A** | What's that? |
| **B** | Lots of angels. |
| **Reader** | . . . a great company of the heavenly host appeared with the angel, praising God and saying: |
| **B** | (*With the Reader*) 'Glory to God in the highest, and on earth peace to those on whom his favour rests!' |

(*The shepherds mime appropriately.*)

| | |
|---|---|
| **Reader** | When the angel had left them and gone into heaven, the shepherds said to one another, 'Let's go to Bethlehem and see this thing that has happened, which the Lord has told us about.' |

(*The shepherds start to move towards the crib, then freeze, as someone carrying a huge Christmas card in front of them comes marching on and takes up position centre stage.*)

| | |
|---|---|
| **Card** | Christmas cards! |
| | (*Recites*) |
| | Post your cards without delay |
| | To all your friends both far and near. |
| | For this is how we all can say: |
| | Merry Christmas, Happy New Year. (*Leaping in the air!*) |
| | Merry Christmas, Happy New Year! |
| **A** | Excuse me! (*Trying even harder to see the crib*) |

(*The Card leaps in the air, shouting, 'Merry Christmas, Happy New Year!', while the Tree comes to life and dances around singing, 'O Christmas tree, O Christmas tree' and the Shopper leaps into life waving her list, shouting, 'Look at my list! Look at my list!'*)

**20**

**A & B**    (*Both straining to see the crib*) Excuse me!

(*The Card, the Tree and the Shopper all freeze.*)

**B**         Thank you! Now can we carry on please?

(*The shepherds go to the crib and kneel beside it, as the reading continues. All the time A and B are trying to peer round those on the stage to see what is happening.*)

**Reader**    So the shepherds hurried off and found Mary and Joseph, and the baby, who was lying in a manger.

(*Two party-goers enter, wearing funny hats, draped in streamers and balloons, cans in their hands, and so on.*)

**Party-goers** It's Christmas! It's partytime! Whee! (*Letting off some party-poppers!*)

It's party-time!

**A**         Excuse me! (*Trying even harder to see the crib*)

(*There is a burst of disco music. The Party-goers dance to it, shouting, 'It's party time!' while the Card, the Tree and the Shopper all come to life and do their individual actions.*)

**A & B**    (*Both straining to see the crib*) Excuse me!

(*The Party-goers, the Card, the Tree and the Shopper all freeze.*)

**B**         Thank you! Now can we carry on please?

(*The shepherds exit during the next reading.*)

**Reader**    The shepherds returned, glorifying and praising God for all the things they had heard and seen . . .

(*In quick succession, three more 'obstructions' come running on and do their bit: Person C, carrying several presents wrapped in Christmas paper; Person D, carrying a Christmas edition of Radio Times; and, finally, Father Christmas, in traditional costume! The stage gets really crowded now and the observers stand up, striving to see Bethlehem through the crowd, eventually finishing up standing on their chairs.*)

**C**         Christmas presents! Whee! (*Starts tearing paper off one of the presents*)

**A**         Excuse me!

**D**         Mary Poppins on the telly! (*Sings and dances*) 'Supercallifragilisticexpialidocious!'

**B**          Excuse me!

**Father C**   And Father Christmas!

**C & D**      Hooray!

**Father C**   Ho-ho-ho! ho-ho-ho!

**A**          Excuse me!

(*Now all the 'obstructions' come to life and do their bit. C unwraps more presents, shouting 'Christmas presents', D sings 'Supercalli . . . etc', Father Christmas goes, 'Ho-ho-ho'. Lots of noise and action on the stage, until . . .*)

**A & B**      (*Top of their voices, now standing on their chairs*) Excuse me!!

(*All the obstructions stop and turn to look at A and B.*)

**Ensemble**   Yes?

**A**          What is going on, please?

**Ensemble**   It's Christmas!

(*In quick succession . . .*)

**Shopper**    Shopping!

**Tree**       Christmas trees!

**Card**       Christmas cards!

**Party-goers**    Party-time!

**C**          Presents!

**D**          Television!

**Father C**   Father Christmas!

**B**          That's all very well, but . . .

**A & B**      (*In unison, very deliberately*) WE CAN'T SEE JESUS!

(*All freeze. Blackout.*)

# It makes you think

## (New Year's Eve)

### Introduction

This sketch simply challenges the audience to think about the implications of the passing of another year of their lives. It raises the question that there must be more to life than just moving along the conveyor belt from one year to another until we die. Rather like most of Ecclesiastes, it does not actually provide any positive Christian answer. But I hope that the sketch could be an interesting and thought-provoking prelude to a talk or discussion about this question. To be effective it requires precise, carefully-rehearsed, rhythmical movements.

### Bible base

*Ecclesiastes 12. 6–7: 'Remember him (your Creator) – before the silver cord is severed . . . and the dust returns to the ground it came from.'*

### Cast

Eleven actors, dressed identically

*This is easier to do than to explain! At the starting point five people line up along the front of the stage, standing absolutely straight with their arms by their sides, facing the front. We will refer to the positions of the five people on the stage at any given time as A, B, C, D and E from stage right to stage left. There should be a space of two to three feet between each of them, with A at the edge of the stage. Throughout the sketch all actors move rhythmically with controlled movements, like robots. The same sequence of movements is repeated seven times, while all the performers chant the seven verses. During each verse they all move along one place, and, apart from in the last verse, the person on the end, stage right (i.e. A), falls off the stage, and another person joins the line on the end, stage left.*

*Each verse requires the following sequence of 22 movements (except the last verse which stops at step 16):*

1.  *E takes one sideways step to the right.*

2.  *E drags the left foot along the floor to meet the right foot and stands upright.*

3.  *E raises right arm vertically, palm facing forwards.*

4.  *E taps D on the head with right hand.*

5.  *E moves right arm back to vertical position. D moves right foot one space sideways.*

6.  *E lowers right arm. D drags the left foot along the floor to meet the right foot and stands upright.*

7.  *D raises right arm vertically, palm facing forwards.*

8.  *D taps C on the head with right hand.*

9.  *D moves right arm back to vertical position. C moves right foot one space sideways.*

10. *D lowers right arm. C drags the left foot along the floor to meet the right foot and stands upright.*

11. *C raises right arm vertically, palm facing forwards.*

12. *C taps B on the head with right hand.*

13. *C moves right arm back to vertical position. B moves right foot one space sideways.*

14. *C lowers right arm. B drags the left foot along the floor to meet the right foot and stands upright.*

15. *B raises right arm vertically, palm facing forwards.*

16. *B taps A on the head with right hand.*

17. *A falls off the edge of the stage, behind a screen, while B raises right arm to vertical and then lowers it. (Have a mattress available to soften A's landing!)*

18. *The four remaining actors make an action as though holding a bell rope moving upwards.*

19. *They pull the imaginary bell rope downwards.*

20. *Arms down again, and move right foot one space to the right.*

**24**

21.    *Drag the left foot to the right, thus arriving in their next starting position.*

22.    *Another performer enters and joins the line on the end, stage left, thus replacing E, who is now D (D is now C, and so on).*

*The numbers in the verses below correspond to the numbers of the movements in the above sequence. The verses are chanted very rhythmically by all the performers (on or off the stage) in a kind of robotic, monotonic voice. There should be a clear gap between one line and the next, with the lines (and accompanying actions) being delivered approximately one every two seconds (except line and action 17 which takes twice as long). We have found it very difficult to remember both the words and the sequence of actions, so it may be a good idea to have someone sitting in front of the actors, holding cue cards from which they can read the lines.*

## Verse 1

| | | | |
|---|---|---|---|
| 1. | Clank. | 2. | Clink. |
| 3. | Clank. | 4. | Clink. |
| 5. | Clank. | 6. | Clink. |
| 7. | It makes | 8. | you think. |
| 9. | Another | 10. | year: |
| 11. | we're on | 12. | the brink. |
| 13. | Clank. | 14. | Clink. |
| 15. | It makes | 16. | you think. |

17.    *(Person A, as they fall)* Aaaah!

       *(A rather feeble, fatalistic cry rather than a dramatic scream)*

| | | | |
|---|---|---|---|
| 18. | Ding. | 19. | Dong. |
| 20. | Move | 21. | along. |
| 22. | *(Pause)* | | |

## Verse 2

| | | | |
|---|---|---|---|
| 1. | Tick. | 2. | Tock. |
| 3. | Tock. | 4. | Tick. |
| 5. | The years | 6. | are passing |

| 7. | very | 8. | quick. |
|---|---|---|---|
| 9. | The date: | 10. | December |
| 11. | thirty | 12. | one. |
| 13. | Another | 14. | year. |
| 15. | What have | 16. | you done? |
| 17. | (*Person A, as they fall*) Aaaah! | | |
| 18. | Ding | 19. | Dong. |
| 20. | Move | 21. | along. |
| 22. | (*Pause*) | | |

## Verse 3
(*Repeat verse 1*)

## Verse 4

| 1. | Advancing | 2. | years |
|---|---|---|---|
| 3. | you may | 4. | be dreading, |
| 5. | but where | 6. | d' you think |
| 7. | your life | 8. | is heading? |
| 9. | The sands | 10. | of time |
| 11. | are running | 12. | fast. |
| 13. | The next | 14. | new year |
| 15. | may be | 16. | your last! |
| 17. | (*Person A, as they fall*) Aaaah! | | |
| 18. | Ding | 19. | Dong. |
| 20. | Move | 21. | along. |
| 22. | (*Pause*) | | |

## Verse 5
(*Repeat verse 1*)

## *Verse 6*

| | | | |
|---|---|---|---|
| 1 | Is this | 2. | what |
| 3. | it's all | 4. | about? |
| 5. | Just live | 6. | until |
| 7. | your time | 8. | runs out? |
| 9. | Four. | 10. | Three. |
| 11. | Two. | 12. | One. |
| 13. | Zero | 14. | hour. |
| 15. | Your time | 16. | has come. |
| 17. | (*Person A, as they fall*) Aaaah! | | |
| 18. | Ding | 19. | Dong. |
| 20. | Move | 21. | along. |
| 22. | (*Pause*) | | |

## *Verse 7*

| | | | |
|---|---|---|---|
| 1 | Tick. | 2. | Tock. |
| 3. | Tock. | 4. | Tick. |
| 5. | The years | 6. | are passing |
| 7. | very | 8. | quick. |
| 9. | Another | 10. | year: |
| 11. | we're on | 12. | the brink. |
| 13. | Clank. | 14. | Clink. |
| 15. | It makes | 16. | you think. |

(*All freeze – A does not fall.   Blackout.*)

# Happy New Year!

## (New Year)

### Introduction

This sketch makes the point that a new year will be simply just another old year without the added ingredient of God's eternal newness.

### Bible base

*Ecclesiastes 1. 9; Ezekiel 36. 26; 2 Corinthians 5. 17; Lamentations 3. 23*

### Cast

Three actors, A, B and C

*A small table is needed on stage to hold various props. Two chairs should also be accessible. The action needs to be very well-rehearsed and extremely slick. A, B and C enter and greet each other, with 'Happy New Year' all round.*

**A, B, C**   *(To audience)*   Happy New Year!

*(They recoil in surprise when the audience respond! They then line up along the front of the stage and adopt thinking poses.)*

**A**   Happy?

**B**   New?

**C**   Year?

**A**   What is a year? *(Stepping to one side and speaking as a scientist)*

   A year is by definition the time taken for the planet earth to complete one elliptical orbit around the sun.

*(While this line is delivered, B sits on a chair and acts as the sun, while C, the earth, does an orbit.)*

**A**   What was that?

C        That was a new year's revolution.

A        That was pathetic. To continue. A year is four seasons: winter . . .

(*B and C shiver.*)

spring . . .

(*B and C spring in the air.*)

summer . . .

(*B and C act as though sunbathing.*)

autumn . . .

(*B and C wiggle their fingers to represent leaves falling, then wrap their arms around themselves, as though getting cold again.*)

A year is twelve months.

(*B picks up and holds up a calendar, while C tears off the pages and throws them away.*)

January, February, March, April, May . . . and the other seven.

(*B throws away the rest of the calendar. A becomes a schoolteacher; B and C get chairs and sit on them facing A, as though pupils, putting up hands eagerly to answer the questions.*)

A        A year is how many weeks? Jones?

C        Fifty-two, sir (*or 'miss'*).

A        Correct. A year is how many days? Smith?

B        Three hundred and sixty-five, sir (*or 'miss'*).

A        Correct. And that is how many hours? Jones?

C        Eight thousand, seven hundred and sixty, sir (*or 'miss'*).

A        Correct. And that is how many minutes? Smith?

B        Five hundred and twenty-five thousand, six hundred, sir (*or 'miss'*).

A        Correct. And that is how many seconds?

(*Turning to the audience*) Audience? (*Back to C*) Jones?

C        Three million, one hundred and fifty-three thousand, six hundred, sir (*or 'miss'*).

A        Correct. So, start counting. Now!

**29**

B        (*Standing with one arm extended, and moving it like the second hand of a clock*)  Tick, tick, tick, tick, tick . . .

C        Oh, golly! What shall I do with three million, one hundred and fifty-three thousand, six hundred seconds?

(*C stands and looks at wrist watch, and mouths counting in time with the ticks: one, two, three, four, five, six . . . then . . .* )

Stop! That's my life ticking away!

A        Stop the clock!

B        (*Carrying on*) Sorry. Tick, tick, tick, tick. Impossible. Tick, tick, tick, tick. You cannot stop time passing. Tick, tick, tick . . . (*continue*)

A        Two hundred and fifty journeys to work.

(*C acts as though driving to work.*)

And two hundred and fifty journeys home again.

(*C acts as though driving home again. Then C sits down and picks up a cup and saucer from the table.*)

One thousand, four hundred and sixty cups of coffee to drink. Three hundred and twelve copies of the *Daily Telegraph* (*or some other appropriate newspaper*) to read.

(*B is still ticking!*)

C        (*Picking up and reading newspaper, delivering lines rapidly*) Same old news. Wars. Disasters. Scandal. Political wrangling. Economic problems. Urban decay. Rural decay. Industrial disputes. England lose a Test Match. Cost of living up. Norwich City down. (*Change this reference to a local football team.*)

A        (*Delivering these lines like a preacher, with extravagant gestures*) 'What has been will be again. What has been done will be done again. There is nothing new under the sun.'

C        That's depressing.

A        That's Ecclesiastes.

C        (*Sitting again and folding arms in a resigned fashion*) This isn't a new year! It's just another old year. Just the same as all the rest.

(*B stops ticking.*)

A        You've stopped!

**B**     My arm was aching.

*(The three line up along the front again during the following lines.)*

**C**     Now's our chance, before the clock gets going again. Question: how do you turn another old year into a happy new year?

**A**     I know how to turn a car into a drive.

**C**     That's pathetic.

**B**     I give up. How do you turn another old year into a happy new year?

**C**     I don't know. That's why I asked.

**A**     We must find . . . *(raising a finger)* . . . the missing ingredient!

**B**     The source of all newness!

**C**     Right, let's think.

*(They all adopt thinking poses. Eventually . . .)*

**C**     Harrods Sale starts on Monday. Would some snappy new gear make a happy new year?

*(They all give it some thought. Then in unison, shaking their heads . . .)*

**A, B, C**  No!

*(They adopt thinking poses again. Then . . .)*

**B**     *(Picking up a holiday brochure from the table)* Would a week in Kashmir make a happy new year?

*(They all give it some thought. Then in unison, shaking their heads . . .)*

**A, B, C**  No!

**A**     *(Picking up a car magazine)* Or a zippy new car?

**B**     *(Still looking at brochure)* Or a trip to Tangier?

**C**     *(Strumming)* A hippie guitar?

**A**     *(Raising arms hopefully)* Or a brand new career?

*(They all give it some thought. Then in unison, shaking their heads . . .)*

**A, B, C**  No!

**A**     *(A little embarrassed)* Actually, I think I know the answer.

**B, C**   You do?!

A        Yes, but I didn't like to mention it.

B, C     Go on . . .

A        What we need is . . . (*spinning once through 360 degrees*) . . . a new year's revolution!

B, C     Go on . . .

A        (*Picking up a Bible and pointing to it*) God's word says: I will give you a new heart and a new spirit.

C        (*Looking downcast, with one hand on heart*) I could do with that.

B        (*Same gesture*) So could I.

C        (*Spins once through 360 degrees, then with head raised high, arms held out, and a confident look on the face*)  A new heart!

B        (*Same action*) A new spirit!

A        If anyone is in Christ they are a new creation.

(*C and B look at themselves and feel themselves all over.*)

A        The old has gone!

(*C and B rush off-stage.*)

A        The new has come!

(*C and B rush on again!*)

C        (*Panting, and as though just having made a great discovery*) The Lord's great love is . . . new . . .

B        (*Likewise*) . . . every morning.

(*They collapse into the chairs. Then they suddenly sit up smartly!*)

B, C     New every morning!

A        (*Returning to schoolteacher mode, with B and C responding as pupils again*) And how many mornings is that? Smith?

B        Three hundred and sixty-five, sir (*or 'miss'*).

A        Correct. And what does that make? Jones?

C        A happy new year, sir (*or 'miss'*)!

A        Correct!

A, B, C  (*Turning to the audience*) Happy New Year! (*Exit*)

# Gardeners' Question Time

## (Education Sunday)

### Introduction

This sketch provides an opportunity to reflect on the challenge of bringing up a child, by analogy with the nurturing of a young plant. It leads to the biblical conclusion that what those who care for children should aim to provide above everything else is 'wisdom'.

### Bible base

*Proverbs 4. 5–7; 9. 10; 22. 6; John 15. 1–2*

### Cast

Mrs Green
Lorna Mower
Bill Flowerbuds
Ivor Greenhouse
Florrie Bunder
Mr Brown
a small boy in a flower pot
two porters to carry him in

*Bill Flowerbuds, Ivor Greenhouse, Florrie Bunder – the Gardeners' Question Time panel – are seated behind a table, with Lorna Mower in the Chair. Bill is very thoughtful and slightly ponderous in his responses. Florrie is madly enthusiastic. Ivor is a bit of a misery. At the start of the sketch, Mr Brown is seated in front of them, holding a large potted plant.*

| | |
|---|---|
| **Lorna** | Good evening and welcome to another edition of Gardeners' Question Time. I'm Lorna Mower and on our panel this evening we have: Bill Flowerbuds. |
| **Bill** | Good evening. |

| | |
|---|---|
| **Lorna** | Ivor Greenhouse. |
| **Ivor** | Hello. |
| **Lorna** | And Florrie Bunder. |
| **Florrie** | Hi there everyone! |
| **Lorna** | Now our first question comes from Mr Brown of Blackheath. Your question to the panel, Mr Brown. |
| **Mr Brown** | (*Holding up the plant*) What's this? And what shall I do with it? |
| **Lorna** | Bill Flowerbuds . . . |
| **Bill** | Ah, this one is easy. It's a buddleia variabilis magnifica. I've got one in my garden. |
| **Florrie** | I've got two. They're absolutely wonderful! |
| **Lorna** | Thank you, Florrie. Ivor Greenhouse, what should Mr Brown do with his buddleia variabilis magnifica? |
| **Ivor** | Chuck it on the compost heap, by the look of it. |
| **Lorna** | Do you agree with that, Bill? |
| **Bill** | No. If you treat it right that'll grow into a handsome shrub. Just plant it in a nice, open, sunny position, in good soil. |
| **Florrie** | Prune it severely every spring. Clip, clip, clip! |
| **Bill** | Give it an annual mulch of rotted horse manure and vegetable compost. |
| **Florrie** | Keep it well watered. Sprinkle, sprinkle, sprinkle. |
| **Bill** | And feed it regularly with a nitrogen, phosphorus and potash fertiliser. |
| **Ivor** | Or chuck it on the compost heap. |
| **Lorna** | Well, there you are Mr Brown. Thank you. Good luck with your buddleia variabilis magnifica. Now, who's next? |

(*Mr Brown exits, Mrs Green enters and sits down.*)

Ah, Mrs Green of Redbridge. Now Mrs Green, what's your problem?

**34**

| | |
|---|---|
| **Mrs Green** | I've got this growing at home. |

(*She indicates behind her. Two porters, wearing brown overalls, enter, carrying between them a small boy with his feet firmly planted in a large flower pot. They stand him in front of the panel and exit.*)

| | |
|---|---|
| **Mrs Green** | I wanted some advice on how best to look after it. |
| **Lorna** | Right. This looks like a tricky one. OK. Over to you, panel. Bill? |
| **Bill** | Ah, yes. I've seen one of these before. A friend of mine had one. |
| **Florrie** | I had two myself. They were absolutely wonderful! Well, some of the time. They can grow quite big, you know. |
| **Ivor** | They can be a bit of a handful as well, if you're not careful. |
| **Mrs Green** | What's it called? Is it a hydrangea? |
| **Bill** | No. Its Latin name is homo sapiens juvenalia. Commonly known as . . . a child. |
| **Ivor** | It's a pretty horrible-looking specimen, isn't it. Do you feed it regularly? |
| **Mrs Green** | Oh, yes. Several times a day, usually. This is what I've given it this week. (*She hands over a list*) |
| **Florrie** | (*Looking at the list*) Mmm . . . Do you think it might do better with a few less chips and chocolate bars? Cut down on the sugar and fat? Increase the fibre and protein content? |

(*The boy in the pot looks suitably disgruntled!*)

| | |
|---|---|
| **Bill** | Now one of the problems with these is that they can run a bit wild and get out of hand. You'll need to be quite strict at times with the pruning. You know, encourage the best bits, but be quite ruthless with anything that's heading in the wrong direction. Remember the old gardener's proverb: 'Train a young plant in the way he should go and when he be old he will not depart from it.' |

**35**

| | |
|---|---|
| Ivor | I'm not too keen on these actually. I wouldn't have one if you gave it to me. They're very susceptible to all kinds of viruses, you know. Can be quite unpleasant. |
| Lorna | Like what? |
| Ivor | Well, the worst is . . . the sulks. |
| Lorna | The sulks? Mmm. Now, what can you do if it gets an attack of the sulks? Bill? |
| Bill | Now, you'll need to spray it liberally with a mixture of patience, tolerance, forgiveness, acceptance, understanding . . . |
| Florrie | . . . and love. |
| Bill | In fact, you're going to need vast quantities of these, so you'd better get stocked up. |
| Lorna | Now what about regular care? Any advice? Florrie . . . |
| Florrie | Well, the other thing you can do is talk to it. |
| Mrs Green | Talk to it? No, you're pulling my leg. Talk to it! |
| Florrie | Yes, I know it sounds a bit far-fetched, but research definitely shows that they do better if you talk to them. |
| Mrs Green | Well, I've heard about people talking to their tomato plants, but I never thought . . . |
| Florrie | Go on, give it a try. Talk to it. Every day. About anything, and everything! Show you care! Show you're interested! |
| Lorna | OK. So, anything else needed? Bill . . . |
| Bill | Well, they're tough these children, but they can get damaged, you know. There are all kinds of things out there ready to attack them. |
| Mrs Green | So, how can I protect it? I mean, I can't be looking after it all the time, can I? I've got my own life to live, you know. |
| Ivor | All it needs, if you ask me, is a regular mulch of the National Curriculum, annual testing for levels of attainment, and a good dose of competitive sports. That'll sort it out. |

| | |
|---|---|
| **Bill** | Well, maybe. But my old gardening book says that what it needs more than anything else . . . is wisdom. If you can give it wisdom, that's what will protect it. Come what may. Whatever else you give your child, Mrs Green, above all, give it wisdom. |
| **Mrs Green** | Wisdom? I wouldn't know where to begin. |
| **Bill** | Well, just remember the old proverb: the fear of the Lord is the beginning of wisdom. |
| **Mrs Green** | Well, I don't know. It all sounds like hard work to me. I think I might take it back and get a hydrangea. |
| **Florrie** | No, don't do that. They really are worth persevering with. They're actually very valuable. |
| **Mrs Green** | So, how much is it worth then? |
| **Ivor** | God knows! |
| **Florrie & Bill** | (*Pointing in Ivor's direction*) Yes! |

# What is this thing called love?

## (St Valentine's Day)

### Introduction

This sketch explores in a humorous fashion some different notions of human love and then contrasts these with the sacrificial love of God, who loved us so much he gave his only Son to die for us.

### Bible base
*I John 3. 16 and 4. 10*

### Cast

All the characters on stage in this sketch are played by four actors, two male (A and C) and two female (B and D), who adopt different roles each time they enter. There is also a voice off-stage.

*At the start of the sketch the four actors enter and line up along the front of the stage, in order, A, B, C, D, from stage right to stage left. Since A and D have bunches of flowers concealed behind their backs, all four stand with their hands behind their backs.*

**All**      (*Chanting in unison*) What is this thing called love?

(*B and C exit opposite sides, B stage right, C stage left. A and D coyly edge closer to each other, then speak and act in unison . . .*)

**A & D**      (*Together, to each other, rather soppily*) I love you! (*Each produces their bunch of flowers*) For you! (*They swap bunches*) For me? Aaah!

(*A and D exit, arm in arm, stage right, as B and C enter from opposite sides. C is wearing a postman's hat and hands an envelope to B as they pass.*)

**38**

C          For you.

B          For me?

(*C exits stage right.*)

B          (*Opening and reading what is clearly a St Valentine's Day card*) 'I . . . love . . . you . . .' He loves me! (*She stands there as though in a daze*)

(*A enters and acts as though driving a car around stage. He makes B jump out of the way and she exits stage left. A stops centre stage, takes out a car magazine, and pronounces his line very intensely . . .*)

A          For me! (*Kissing the magazine in exaggerated fashion*) Mm! I love you!

(*A drives off stage left, as D and B enter, B from stage left, D from stage right. D sings the first line of 'Happy Birthday to You'.*)

D          (*Handing over a ten-pound note*) For you-hoo!

B          (*Accepting it, but disappointed at this expression of 'love'*) For me? Thanks.

(*D exits stage left, calling out, in a shallow, insincere manner, as he goes . . .*)

D          Love you.

B          (*Looking disappointed*) Oh, um . . . yeah . . . love you!

           (*Studying the note*) Love?

(*B walks off stage right, as C enters, looking at himself in a mirror, adjusting his hair, admiring himself from different angles . . .*)

C          (*Talking to himself*) Oh, I love you! I love you! I love you!

(*C crosses the stage and exits stage left, as A and D enter, arm in arm. They are now a much older couple than before.*)

A          (*Pompously*) Darling . . . I . . . er . . . prompt!

**Off-stage**   (*Whispered loudly*) Love . . . you . . .

A          Oh, yes . . . (*pompously again*) Darling . . . I love you.

D          For you!

(*D gives A a stage-punch and flattens him! She then walks to to the right edge of the stage and stands motionless.*)

A          (*Just raising his head and rubbing his jaw*) For me?

**39**

*(A collapses and stays motionless on the ground, to the left of the stage. C enters, wearing a dog-collar. He points to various members of the audience as he walks across stage, carefully stepping over A.)*

**C**     *(In a mock pious voice)* I love you, and you, and you, and you . . .

*(He joins D and stands motionless as though in conversation with her. B rushes on and stands centre stage, waving as though at a train which is just departing. Her eyes follow the imaginary train as it disappears into the distance . . .)*

**B**     *(Shouting)* Bye! . . . I love you! . . . *(quietly and sadly)* I love you . . .

*(She freezes)*

*(There is a loud drum crash. A stands.)*

**A, B, C, D** *(To each other)* What is this thing called love?

*(All four turn to the back of the stage and fall to their knees. All the lights go down. The voice of God is heard . . .)*

**Off-stage**  I love you.

**A, B, C, D** What is love?

*(A silhouette of a cross is projected at the back of the stage.)*

**Off-stage**  This is how we know what love is.

**A, B, C, D** This . . . is love?

**Off-stage**  This is love. Not that we loved God, but that he loved us and gave his one and only Son . . .

**A, B, C, D** For us?

**Off-stage**  For you.

*(Freeze. Pause. Blackout.)*

# As a mother . . .

## (*Mothering Sunday*)

## Introduction

This sketch sets out to remind the audience that the Bible teaches us that God is not just like a father to us, but also in some ways is like a mother. It is dedicated to my own mother, who has always had the mother's knack of knowing when something was upsetting me; who never failed to write her weekly letter when I was at university or working overseas; who always encouraged all four of her children to make the most of their gifts and of life's opportunities; and who, together with my father, taught me the meaning of sacrificial love.

## Bible base

*Genesis 1. 27; Isaiah 49. 14–15; Isaiah 66. 13*

## Cast

Mum
Dad
Jo (daughter)
Harry (son)

*Dad, Mum and daughter, Jo, are sitting round the kitchen table. There are two sons: Jack, who is away at college, and Harry, who is off-stage. Dad is reading a newspaper. Mum is writing a letter to Jack. Dad is bigoted and self-opinionated and annoys everyone by reading bits out of the newspaper.*

**Dad**    Here, listen to this. It says here that the Bishop of Great Snoring (*or use a local reference to a non-existent bishop*) has announced that he doesn't believe any more in heaven, hell, the Resurrection, the Virgin Birth, miracles, creation, the authority of the Bible, the second coming, or the Holy Spirit.

**41**

| | |
|---|---|
| Jo | (*Long-suffering, trying to ignore him*) Really, Dad? |
| Dad | But on the positive side, he is against women priests. |
| Jo | Oh, so that's all right then, eh? |
| Mum | Don't be rude to your father, Jo. He's entitled to his opinions. |
| Jo | But do we have to listen to them all the time? |
| Dad | (*Back in his newspaper*) I don't believe it! This is your barmy European parliament for you. They're bringing in new regulations to standardise the size and shape of cornflakes. Of all the stupid ideas! |
| Mum | You shouldn't read that paper. |

(*Dad ignores her.*)

| | |
|---|---|
| | It only gets you upset. |
| Jo | It ought to carry a government health warning. Danger, reading this paper can seriously damage your equilibrium. |
| Mum | His was damaged years ago! |

(*Mum and Jo laugh.*)

| | |
|---|---|
| Dad | (*Looking up*) What's that? What'd you say? |
| Jo | We were just saying, you shouldn't believe everything you read in the papers, Dad. |
| Dad | (*Going back to his reading*) Norwich City lost again (*or your local team*). Three-nil at home. Call themselves a football team . . . |
| Jo | What're you doing, Mum? |
| Mum | I'm writing to Jack. |
| Dad | I don't know why you bother. He never replies. |
| Jo | When you're away at college it's nice to get some post. |
| Mum | Anyway, I want him to know we don't forget about him, just because he's away from home. |
| Dad | (*Back to his newspaper*) Now listen to this latest bit of nonsense. Someone's brought out (*sneering*) an equal opportunities Bible. Would you believe it! 'Our Father and Mother which art in heaven . . .' Honestly, what is the world coming to? |

| | |
|---|---|
| **Jo** | I don't see what's so wrong with that, actually. |
| **Dad** | What's wrong with that? What's wrong with it, my girl, is that God is our Father. Not our Mother. Here, you get that proper Bible from over there and show me where it says that God is our mother? |
| **Jo** | (*Picking up a Bible*) I know that God is always *called* our Father, but that's only language. He isn't actually male, is he? I mean he isn't actually a man . . . |
| **Dad** | Course he is. He has to be a man. (*Leaning back and putting his feet up on the table*) 'Cause it's we men who are in charge, isn't it. It's men who've got . . . you know . . . authority. |
| **Mum** | You get your feet off that table. |
| **Dad** | (*Compliant*) Sorry, dear. |
| **Jo** | So, what about this then? It says here in Genesis . . . (*looking in the Bible*) . . . in the *proper* Bible . . . 'God made man in his own image . . .' |
| **Dad** | Right. Man. Not wooo . . . man . . . |
| **Jo** | Yes, but 'man' obviously means 'Mankind', human beings generally. Because, listen, it goes on, 'Male and female he created *them*. In the image of God he created *them*.' So if both male and female were made in the image of God then God must be . . . |
| **Dad** | Never mind about that. It says God is our Father and that's good enough for me. We don't need any of this 'Our Father and Mother in heaven' stuff, thank you very much. |

(*Enter Harry, looking a bit miserable. He slumps down at the table next to Mum.*)

| | |
|---|---|
| **Harry** | You two arguing again. |
| **Dad** | This sister of yours is trying to persuade me that God is a woman. |
| **Jo** | No, I didn't say that. I just think it's quite helpful sometimes to think of God being *like* a mother to us . . . (*She turns the pages of the Bible*) |

| | |
|---|---|
| **Mum** | (*Finishing the letter and putting it in the envelope*) There, that's finished that. Now what's up with you, Harry? |
| **Harry** | Oh, nothing, Mum. |
| **Jo** | Like it says here in the Bible: 'Can a mother forget her baby . . . ? In the same way God cannot forget us . . .' |
| **Mum** | (*To Jo*) Just pop that letter in the post for me, will you, Jo? Your brother will get it in the morning then. |
| **Jo** | OK, Mum. |

(*She exits, but takes the Bible with her. Dad goes back to his paper.*)

| | |
|---|---|
| **Mum** | (*To Harry*) Something's up, isn't it? |
| **Harry** | No. Just got rather a lot of homework to do. |
| **Mum** | Come on. What is it? Has she dumped you? |
| **Harry** | You always know, don't you! We can't hide anything from you. |
| **Mum** | Well, I am your mother, Harry. Look, never mind about that silly girl. Her loss is some other girl's gain. Cheer up. I'll make you bread and butter pudding for your tea. (*She puts her arm round him*) I know it feels bad now, Harry, but give it a few days . . . Some girls don't know when they're well off, if you ask me. |

(*Jo returns and confronts Dad with the Bible.*)

| | |
|---|---|
| **Jo** | And look at this, then. See what God says in your Bible: 'As a mother comforts her children so will I comfort you . . .' |
| **Mum** | Give it a rest, Jo. You know you'll never win. |
| **Jo** | But I'm right, aren't I! It's just as true to say that God is like a mother to us as to say he's like a father. |
| **Dad** | Listen to your mother, Jo. Give it a rest. |
| **Mum** | Look, I don't want any arguments today. Not today. |
| **Dad** | What's special about today then? |
| **Mum** | You've forgotten, haven't you? |
| **Dad** | Come on, what is it? |

*(Mum folds her arms and looks upwards, not prepared to help him out.)*

Oh, no, it's not our wedding anniversary, is it?

*(Mum shakes her head. He begins to panic. Jo starts to whistle 'Happy Birthday to You . . .')*

Not your birthday!

*(Mum shakes her head again.)*

Phew! Oh crumbs. What have I forgotten now? It can't be Christmas. I mean, there'd be a tree and everything. Um . . .

*(Jo and Harry get up and go to where they have some gifts hidden.)*

Do you two know what she's talking about?

**Jo**       Might do.

**Dad**      Come on, give us a clue.

**Harry**    All right then. How about this? *(He produces a bunch of flowers from behind his back)*

**Jo**       And this! *(She produces a box of chocolates)*

**Harry**    *(To Mum)* We love you, Mum.

**Jo**       Thanks for being Mum.

**Jo & Harry**   *(Together, presenting the gifts with exaggerated gestures)* Happy Mother's Day!

# Peter's denial

## (Lent/Maundy Thursday)

### Introduction

This sketch is a simple modern-day parallel to Peter's denial of his allegiance to the Lord Jesus. It is not particularly profound, but aims to use a modern-day scene simply to introduce the ideas of loyalty and failure to be loyal when under pressure. It was written to be used with a group of young people as an introduction to a discussion of the biblical account of Peter's denial.

### Bible base

*John 18. 15–18, 25–27*

### Cast

Peter
Café owner
Bystanders 1 and 2

*There is an area of the stage representing a café, with a counter and a few chairs around a table. The café owner is behind the counter. Bystander 1 is seated at the table. A young football fan called Peter enters. He is wearing an anorak, and looking decidedly fed up. He has just come from an away match that his team has lost. The name of the football team should be changed as appropriate to local circumstances.*

| | |
|---|---|
| **Peter** | Well, that's it. Ipswich Town relegated. That's the last twenty matches they've lost. And I've been there for every one! Well, at least no-one can accuse me of not being loyal! I've stuck with them right through. But it's all over now. Down we go. And we had such high hopes at the start of the season . . . Brrr, it was cold at the match this afternoon. I'm just going to pop into this café and drown my sorrows in a cup of tea. |

(*He goes into the café.*)

**Café owner**    Here, you're not one of them Ipswich Town supporters are you?

**Peter**    Sorry? What's that?

**Café owner**    You're not an Ipswich fan are you? We don't want no football hooligans in here, thank you very much.

**Peter**    Um, no. Not me. No. I'll just have a cup of tea, thanks.

**Café owner**    All right then. But no trouble, right? OK, here's your tea. Forty pence, please.

(*Appropriate action.*)

**Peter**    Thanks. (*Warming his hands on the cup*) Brrr, it's cold out there today.

**Bystander 1**    You're not from around here are you? That's a Suffolk accent isn't it?

**Peter**    Um . . .

**Bystander 1**    I bet you're an Ipswich Town fan! (*Mocking*)

Ha, ha, ha! Pity about the result . . . (*Chanting*)

Five-nil, five-nil, five-nil, five-nil . . . Ipswich Town, going down!

**Peter**    No, I'm not! I'm not interested in football, thank you. I'm . . . just up here on business.

(*Bystander 2 enters during the above exchange and buys a cup of tea from the counter. He then turns to Peter.*)

**Bystander 2**    Didn't I see you at the match this afternoon? That's right. You were standing all on your own in the North stand, waving a blue and white scarf!

(*Peter is getting increasingly anxious and embarrassed.*)

**Café owner**    Ho, ho! Ladies and gentleman, we present the last-surviving Ipswich Town fan!

**Bystander 1**    Go on, undo your anorak . . . I bet there's an Ipswich Town scarf under there . . .

**47**

**Peter**    (*Furious*) For the last time, I do not support Ipswich Town! I'm not interested in Ipswich Town. I don't even care about Ipswich Town, and I've had enough of your stupid remarks. And this tea is disgusting. You can keep it, thank you. Good-bye. (*Exit in a temper*)

# On trial

## (*Good Friday*)

## Introduction

This sketch recounts the trial of Jesus by Pontius Pilate – or should it be the trial of Pontius Pilate by Jesus? To get over the difficulties of having someone play the part of Jesus the trial is relived in Pilate's memory, with Pilate talking to an empty chair in which he imagines Jesus is sitting.

## Bible base

*Matthew 27. 11–31; Mark 15. 1–15; Luke 23. 1–25; John 18. 28—19. 24*

## Cast

Pilate
Pilate's Wife
Official

*Pontius Pilate is pacing anxiously around his palace. There is a large, high-backed chair, centre stage, facing away from the audience, with a purple cloak draped over the back of it. Facing the chair is a rostrum from which Pilate delivers his lines when he is reliving the trial. The Official is standing to one side, motionless, facing away from the audience. Pilate's wife enters.*

| | |
|---|---|
| **Wife** | Husband, you've been up since before daybreak and you have not eaten all day. Come, take some food. |
| **Pilate** | I'm sorry. I am deeply disturbed. I cannot get that man out of my mind. |
| **Wife** | I warned you to have nothing to do with him, didn't I? |
| **Pilate** | (*Irritated, because he's heard all this before*) Yes, I know. You had a bad dream about him last night. But what could I do? I am the governor of this province. I could not just wash my hands of the whole affair. |

| Wife | (*Aside*) In the end that is precisely what you did. But by then it was too late. (*To Pilate*) Look, forget about it. It's all over now. I'll get the servants to prepare some food for you. Try to get a little rest . . . (*Exit*) |
|---|---|
| Pilate | (*To himself*) Rest? Huh! How can I rest? I must go over it all again in my mind. I must be sure that I do not bear the guilt for this innocent man's death. Now, let me think. He just sat there in that chair, looking at me . . . |

(*He switches style: he is now reliving the trial, imagining Jesus sitting in the chair; he takes up his position at the rostrum and speaks to the Official, who suddenly comes to life.*)

What is the name of this prisoner? (*Pointing to the chair*)

| Official | (*Reading from a scroll*) Jesus. |
|---|---|
| Pilate | Who brings a charge against him? |
| Official | The council of Jewish elders, your Excellency. They're outside. Won't come in. Don't want to be defiled by setting foot on Gentile property. You, know, it's their Passover thing. |
| Pilate | So, what is the charge against this man? |
| Official | Um . . . (*Reading in a matter-of-fact manner*) . . . subverting the nation. Opposing payment of taxes to Caesar. Claiming to be the Son of God. Claiming to be the Christ. Oh, and, er, claiming to be a King. The council asks you to sentence him to death. Usual arrangement, governor? |
| Pilate | (*He keeps looking at the chair*) One moment . . . (*Walking across to face the chair*) So, you are the King of the Jews? Right? (*Pause*) |
| | Mm? Are you not going to say anything to defend yourself? Look, it is your own people that are bringing this charge against you. What is it that you have done that upsets them so much? Ah, you Jews. You're always causing trouble. (*He pauses, as though listening*) What? (*To the Official*) What does he mean, his Kingdom is of another place? |
| Official | Don't ask me. I'm out of my depth. |
| Pilate | (*To the chair again*) So, you are a King then? Yes? (*Mockingly*) |

**50**

Oh, thank you. (*To the Official*) Did you hear that? He says I speak the truth. Huh! (*To the chair*) What is truth? Are these charges true? Are they false? Who knows?

**Official**   Who cares!

**Pilate**   Look, I'm inclined to let you go. (*To the Official*) Tell the Jewish leaders I find no basis for the charge against him. Take him away.

**Official**   They, um, won't like that, your Excellency. They're really worked up over this one. Could have a riot on your hands. We could lose control. Look, better to let this one man die for the sake of the whole nation. They say he's been causing trouble all over, ever since he came down from Nazareth.

**Pilate**   But what exactly has he done? (*To the chair*) Look, what is going on here? I can't see what you've done that's so awful. But they want your blood. And I've got to keep the peace somehow. What can I do? (*Suddenly turning to the Official*) Did you say Nazareth?

**Official**   Yes . . .

**Pilate**   (*To the chair*) Ah, so, you're from Galilee. Excellent. (*To the Official*) In that case he comes under Herod's jurisdiction. Who just happens to be in Jerusalem today. There . . . (*To the chair*) Herod can decide your fate . . . (*To the Official*) Take him away . . .

(*quietly, as though trying to get Jesus out of his mind*)

. . . take him away . . .

(*The Official turns away from the audience and again stands motionless; Pilate reverts to the present, again talking to himself.*)

I did try, didn't I? And even Herod agreed with me. Huh, first time we've seen eye to eye for years!

(*Pilate's wife enters.*)

**Wife**   Are you still going on about that man? Look, it's over now. The sentence is passed . . .

**Pilate**   But, I did try. I called all the Jewish leaders together and told them. There was no basis for the charge against him. Herod and I had agreed. He'd done nothing to deserve death. I offered to have him beaten to teach him a lesson. But they wouldn't have it. They wouldn't settle for anything less than his death.

**Wife**　Come, Pilate, your meal is prepared . . . (*Exit*)

**Pilate**　I did everything I could, didn't I?

(*He reverts to reliving the trial: he speaks to the Official, who comes to life again.*)

Is there no way out of this mess?

**Official**　Well, your Excellency, it is the custom for the governor to release one prisoner at the time of the Passover. You could try that.

**Pilate**　Oh, yes. Of course. Ask them if they want me to release this 'King of the Jews'.

(*Exit Official.*)

(*To the chair*) What is going on here? Tell me. Why is it so important to them that you should die? Eh? Where do you come from? Who are you? (*Getting angry*) Come on, say something!

(*Official returns. Pilate speaks to him.*)

Now he refuses to speak to me. I could almost believe that, for some reason, he accepts that he must die. So, what did they say?

**Official**　(*Quietly*) Barabbas . . .

**Pilate**　Barabbas! That thug!

**Official**　I know. But that's what they say. 'Not him . . . (*indicating the chair*) . . . give us Barabbas.'

**Pilate**　So what should I do with this Jesus?

**Official**　Listen to them out there . . . There's your answer . . . Can't you hear it? The chanting . . .

**Pilate**　(*As though listening at a window*) Crucify, crucify, crucify . . . What is going on here? He sits here in silence like a sheep waiting to be sheared, while that lot out there are baying for his blood. (*To the chair*) Is this what you want? To be nailed to a cross like a common criminal? Answer me, man! Don't you realise that I have power to set you free or to have you crucified?

(*To the Official*) I cannot send this innocent man to Golgotha. I have made up my mind. I will let him go.

**Official**  The Jews are saying that if you let him you go you will be no friend of Caesar.

**Pilate**  Caesar? Why should he care about this Jew?

**Official**  The Jewish leaders will tell Caesar that he claimed to be a King, and anyone who claims to be a King opposes Caesar. And Caesar will ask who ordered his release . . .

**Pilate**  (*Giving up*) I'm trapped, aren't I. Either he dies or I'm ruined. All right. Hand him over to them. Let them crucify their 'King'. (*To the chair*) But just tell me one thing, will you? You're nobody. Just a preacher from Galilee, with a small crowd of followers. Even your own people have rejected you. And me . . . I'm the Roman Governor of this province. The most powerful man in the region. So how come that my whole future seems to depend on what I do with you? What is going on here?

(*Official exits, as Pilate's wife enters.*)

**Wife**  What is done cannot be undone. Stop tormenting yourself, husband.

**Pilate**  (*Reverting to the present again*) Yes, all right. I will come and eat.

(*The Official enters, carrying a rectangular piece of wood. Pilate's wife appears to be looking out of the window.*)

**Official**  Your Excellency, this notice you asked to be fastened to the cross: Jesus of Nazareth, the King of the Jews. The Jewish leaders have complained. They say it should read: this man claimed to be the King of the Jews . . .

**Pilate**  (*Angrily*) What I have written, I have written!
(*Thoughtfully*) What I have written, I have written.

**Wife**  Look, there goes that murderer, Barabbas.

**Pilate**    (*Joining her at the window*) Well at least one sinner has bene-
fited from this innocent man's death. Look, the sun is directly
overhead now. It is the sixth hour. He will be crucified by
now . . .

(*The lights gradually go down.*)

The sun! Look at it . . . The sun is . . . dying! What is happening here? What is going on?

(*The Official and the wife look terrified, as the darkness descends and Pilate sinks
to his knees and cries out . . .*)

O God, what have I done!
(*Then quietly*) O God, what have you done?

# Garden path

## (*Easter Sunday*)

### Introduction

In this sketch I have tried to imagine what it might have been like for the gardener looking after Joseph's garden during the events of the first Easter. The sketch is almost a monologue as the gardener sets the scene, recounts the incidents of Good Friday and responds to the events of Easter Sunday – until Mary meets him and tells him about her meeting with the risen Lord Jesus.

### Bible base

*The Gospel accounts of the death and, especially, the Resurrection of the Lord Jesus: Matthew 27–28; Mark 15–16; Luke 23–24; John 19–20. Also Genesis 8. 22 and John 12. 24*

### Cast

The Gardener
Three women, including Mary Magdalene
Peter and John

*The scene is Joseph of Arimathea's garden. The time is early on the first Easter Sunday morning. The gardener enters, potters about and chats to the audience. He is carrying a rake and a net of oranges. He should have a low stool to sit on from time to time, as appropriate. Along the front of the stage is an imaginary bed where he has planted some radishes. This is the basis for an ongoing joke throughout the sketch as various players in the story run backwards and forwards across his radish bed!*

**Gardener**   Sunday morning. Peace and quiet at last. This is my garden, you see. Well, not exactly mine. I'm just the gardener. Belongs to my master, Joseph. Just on the edge of the city of Jerusalem. Lovely place to come away from the noise and bustle of the city. You can enjoy God's creation in a garden like this. Olives and figs to eat, growing over there (*gesturing to the left*). Flowers and trees, just to look at and enjoy (*gesturing to the right*).

(*He sits down, facing the audience.*) Look at these!

(*He holds up the oranges.*) I've just been picking these oranges, from my orange tree. It's a constant miracle, isn't it! Look, see that.

(*He holds up an orange pip.*) Know what that is? It's an orange pip. Well, I planted one of these over there when I was a lad. And now, well, there's all these oranges. One little orange pip. Looks totally dead and lifeless. But you bury it deep into the ground. And then God sends the rain and the sun, and before you know what, it springs into life!

(*He gets a bit philosophical.*) It makes you think, though, doesn't it. You know, the way God goes on bringing new life. The way he provides what we need. What is it the old scriptures say? (*Struggling a little to recall the text*) 'As long as the earth endures . . . seedtime and harvest . . . cold and heat . . . summer and winter . . . day and night . . . will never cease.' Every year it happens. Just like he promised. And yet there are still people who live their lives as though he doesn't exist. Never bother even to thank him for it all.

Look at this great world he created . . . (*gesturing expansively . . . and then with a little sadness*) . . . pity about the way people spoil it though. With their greed and their selfishness. Jealousy. Hatred. Cruelty.

We've seen plenty of that this last weekend in Jerusalem. Hasn't been much peace and quiet in this garden these last few days, I can tell you. Just when I needed somewhere restful to go, what with it being Passover weekend, and the city packed with visitors.

(*He does a bit of pottering around the garden.*)

I always enjoy the festival of Passover. Every year our family gets together and we remember how God provided for his people when they were slaves in Egypt. So, I think to myself. All right, it's pretty bad at times here with the Romans in charge and so much corruption and cruelty and disturbance. But God looked after his people then, and so I reckon he'll look after us now.

And one day . . . one day, Messiah will come. One day, God will send his chosen one to help his people. He'll sort things out. Every Passover I tell myself this. Some of us were beginning to wonder if that new teacher – Jesus from Nazareth – whether he might be . . . Well, you know, when he told people about God's Kingdom and said that he had come to bring us to our Father in heaven . . . it made you think. But, no, it wasn't to be. They killed him, you know. Friday it was. Hung him up on a cross, on that hill over there (*gesturing behind him*), with a couple of common criminals. So that was the end of him.

(*Sudden change in mood*) Do you like radishes? Love 'em, myself. I planted some radish seeds just along here a week or two ago (*indicating the radish bed*). But it'll be a miracle if I get any radishes after what they've been through.

(*He sits down and goes into narrative mode.*) It all started on Friday evening. First my master turned up. He comes running into the garden. Right across where I planted my radishes (*indicating the radish bed with a sweep of the hand*). In a terrible state. Tears running down his face. He was a follower of that Jesus, you see. Anyway, he says, 'Come along, gardener, get my tomb ready.' Over there (*pointing stage right*), his tomb, for when he dies. He's a rich man. He'll be buried in his garden. So, I'm thinking, has he had bad news from the doctor, or what? Anyway, I do what he says, and he charges off. Right across my radishes again (*indicating the radish bed again*). Then, a bit later, he comes back, with a friend of his. Nicodemus. And it's getting dark now, so I can't quite see what's going on. But they're carrying this huge bundle all wrapped in cloth. Like a dead weight, it was. Right across my radishes again.

**57**

*(Beginning to sound exasperated at the treatment of his radishes!)*.

And they took it down there to the tomb. And I'm wondering what's going on. And my master, he's saying, 'Hurry, Nicodemus, the day of preparation for the Passover is nearly at an end . . . We must get him laid to rest this evening.' And then all of a sudden I realise! It was the body of that Jesus. They had actually carried the dead body of Jesus down from the cross *(indicating the locations)*, down the hill, along that little path . . . and there they were burying him in my master's tomb. In my garden! Well, I could hardly believe it.

So, off they go. Right across my radishes again. And I think, well, it'll be quiet now. I'll just see if I can repair the radish bed. Then, would you believe it, these Roman soldiers turn up. And they're looking around the edge of the garden. Then one of them points to this large boulder, this great big round rock that had fallen over there when we had that earthquake on Friday afternoon. What, didn't I mention the earthquake? I tell you, it has not been a peaceful weekend. So, he says, 'Right, that'll do.' So, I'm thinking, what are they going to do with that? I might have guessed . . . they're going to roll it right across my radishes, aren't they! Down to the tomb. And they're sealing the tomb with it. And I tell you, it's absolutely huge, this boulder. Took four grown men to push it into place. So, I think, well no-one's going to get in there in a hurry. And this Roman officer says, 'Right, you two, keep guard, we don't want his disciples coming in the night and stealing the body.' And then, the rest of them all lined up and marched off, left, right, left, right, left . . . right across my radishes again.

So that was Friday for you. Well, I just raked the radish bed over. Ever hopeful. And went home. What a day!

The next day was our Sabbath, of course. And the beginning of Passover, so, I was at home with the family, with my feet up.

Well, this morning, I thought, I'll get to work early and sort the garden out a bit. See if I can rescue the radishes. Huh! Some hope after what they'd been through. So, here I am, up bright and early on a Sunday morning, not long after sunrise. And would you believe it, look, there are three sets of fresh footprints right across the radish bed! Heading towards the tomb. So, I'm just wondering what is going on here now?

*(Suddenly, there is a commotion from over by the tomb, off-stage right; the three women coming screaming past the gardener. One of the women shouts, 'They've taken him away! They've taken him away!' They run across the radish bed and exit in a hurry, stage left.)*

**Gardener** *(Calling after them)* Here, mind where you're treading! Excuse me . . .

*(Then to the audience)* Look, did you see that? Right across my radishes again.

What is going on over there? Here, I'm going to take a look. Excuse me for a moment.

*(He creeps over to stage right and acts as though peeping through some bushes. He comes back to centre stage, looking perplexed.)*

Well, I don't know whether I should have done that, but I've just been and had a look at the tomb. Here, listen to this. The guards have gone. And the stone, that huge boulder, it's been rolled away. Well, it couldn't have been the women that did it. Much too heavy for them to move it. Anyway, I could just about see inside the tomb. A bit creepy, really. But, you'll never believe this. The body. It's gone. The burial cloths are still there. The linen that was wrapped round the body, and the cloth that was around his head. But no body. Well, it makes you think, doesn't it.

*(He returns to pottering around the garden. Suddenly, there's another commotion, from stage left. John comes tearing across the stage, heading for the tomb. He is closely followed by Peter, and then by Mary Magdalene. Each of them runs straight through the radish bed and exits stage right. The gardener watches like a spectator at Wimbledon, shouting, 'Excuse me . . .' and pointing, as each one runs across his precious radishes!)*

**Gardener** Well, honestly. Look at that! Right across my radishes, again. I give up . . . *(He sits down, looking hopeless.)*

(*Peter and John enter from stage right, talking excitedly. They cross the stage behind the gardener.*)

**Peter**   (*As they cross the stage*) Do you remember now? What he said . . . about the third day . . .

**John**   Yes, of course, it all makes sense now.

**Gardener**   (*As Peter and John exit stage left*) Well, it doesn't make sense to me.

(*Then shouting after them*) Excuse me, but you seem to have forgotten to trample all over my radishes!

(*To the audience*) Just my little joke.

(*Mary enters now from stage right. She comes up to the gardener, looks at him and starts laughing!*)

**Gardener**   You all right, miss? It wasn't that funny, was it?

**Mary**   (*Still laughing*) I thought he was you! Isn't that ridiculous! I thought he was you!

**Gardener**   Who you talking about, miss? There's no-one else in this garden, as far as I know.

**Mary**   But I saw him. Alive! I saw the Lord! Jesus, my master. And I spoke to him. And he spoke to me. And I thought he was you!

(*She starts to exit, still laughing*) I thought he was you!

**Gardener**   (*To the audience*) Well, I don't know much. I'm only a gardener, but I know this. That man was dead.

(*Mary now stops at the edge of the stage, listening.*)

He was buried. His dead body was sealed in that tomb. And here is this woman saying she's just seen him alive. And she thought he was me! Honestly!

(*He sits and looks down at the radish bed. Then he suddenly points excitedly and gets down on his knees to look more closely.*)

Well, look at that! I don't believe it! A blooming miracle. Look! Just bursting through the hard, dry ground, there's a little green shoot! One of my radishes is actually alive! Look at that!

(*Mary comes across as he talks, looking pensive. She stands beside him and looks over his shoulder.*)

**Mary**      Now I understand what he meant.

**Gardener**  What's that?

**Mary**      When we were travelling to Jerusalem, just last week. He told us that a seed must fall to the ground and be buried before it can come back to life again and grow into a plant with many seeds. Just like your radish! Do you see that? It all makes sense now, doesn't it! (*She exits*) Yes, it all makes sense now.

**Gardener**  (*To the audience*) Now she's saying it all makes sense. Well, I don't know. Sounds like a riddle to me. All I know is that I thought my radishes were dead, but, look, they're alive! And that's a little miracle, as far as I'm concerned.

(*He gets up and speaks thoughtfully.*) Mind you, if that Jesus really is alive again . . . well that would be a miracle that could change the world. I mean if a dead man has really come back to life . . . well, it makes you think doesn't it. (*Picking up his things and making his exit*) It makes you think.

# Not the end

## (*Ascension Day*)

### Introduction

In this sketch I have tried to imagine the conversation between the apostles and the women when the apostles returned to the upper room after witnessing the Ascension. This is simply a device to recount the details of this immensely significant event. The sketch makes the point that the return of the Lord to heaven was not the end of his ministry, but was, in a sense, a new beginning, as responsibility was passed from him to the disciples, who, in a few days' time, would receive the empowerment of the Holy Spirit.

### Bible base

*Luke 24. 50–53; Acts 1. 1–14; Philippians 2. 10–11.*

### Cast

Peter
Andrew
James
John
Thomas
Mary Magdalene
Joanna

*Mary Magdalene and Joanna are sitting in the upper room waiting for the apostles to return. Peter, Andrew, James, John and Thomas enter. The women immediately leap up, usher them in, get them chairs, sit them down. As they tell their story, each of the apostles cannot wait to say their bit. The story gets told in short phrases, with each one jumping in quickly to take over.*

| Mary | Come on in. Sit down. You look exhausted. |
| Joanna | We thought you'd never come back! We've been waiting for hours! |
| Peter | It was a long walk back to the city from the Mount of Olives. |
| Mary | Here, refresh yourselves, brothers. (*She pours out drinks for them and passes them round, as the dialogue continues*) |
| Joanna | So? Tell us all. |
| Peter | Well, it was amazing! |
| Andrew | Unbelievable. |
| James | Stunning. |
| John | Awe-inspiring. |
| Thomas | Incredible. |

(*Mary and Joanna sit and listen intently.*)

| Joanna | Don't just work your way through the Thesaurus! Come on, tell us what happened! |
| Peter | Well, he led us out to the Mount of Olives. |
| Andrew | We knew something special was going to happen, but we had no idea. |
| James | (*In a tone which concedes the stupidity of the question*) |
| | We asked if he was going to restore the kingdom of Israel, here and now. |
| John | But he said the Father had set a time for this and it was not for us to know. |
| Thomas | After that we didn't ask any more questions. |
| Peter | We just watched. |
| Andrew | And listened. |
| James | So there we were, all gathered round him . . . |

(*Now they slow down.*)

| John | . . . and he lifted up his hands . . . (*standing and acting appropriately*) . . . like this, and blessed us. |

**Thomas**     And then . . .

*(They all stand now and face away from the women. They hold out their hands and slowly move them upwards, while also slowly raising their heads and looking upwards, as they recall the experience of the Lord's ascension.)*

**Peter**     . . . he was taken up . . . into heaven.

*(They hold their pose, looking up into the heavens, arms held aloft.)*

**Andrew**     We saw it with our own eyes.

**James**     And a cloud hid him from our sight.

**John**     And he was gone.

**Thomas**     Returned to heaven, to the right hand of God the Father.

*(They hold their pose for a few seconds, then fall to their knees, closing their eyes and adopting an attitude of worship. The women suddenly change from looking awe-struck to being extremely anxious.)*

**Joanna**     Gone?

**Mary**     For ever?

*(The disciples get up now and gather round the women, some standing, some sitting.)*

**Joanna**     What, will we never see him again?

**Mary**     As we have seen him these last forty days?

**Joanna**     Is it now, really . . . all over?

**Mary**     Is this . . . the end?

**Peter**     Yes, he is gone. But we're all still here.

*(Gathering pace.)*

**Andrew**     And he gave us a promise, before he went.

**James**      He said we were to wait here in Jerusalem.

**John**     Just for a few days.

**Thomas**     Until he sends the gift from heaven.

**Peter**     He said we are to be baptised . . .

**Andrew**     Not with water . . .

**James**     But with the Holy Spirit!

| | |
|---|---|
| **John** | And we will receive power to take over his work. |
| **Thomas** | To be his witnesses, here in Jerusalem. |
| **Peter** | Throughout Judea. |
| **Andrew** | Samaria. |
| **James** | To the ends of the earth! |
| **John** | So, you see, it isn't the end. |
| **Thomas** | It's just the beginning! |
| (*Pause.*) | |
| **Peter** | And one day, we will see him again. |
| **Joanna** | We will? |
| **Andrew** | There were these two angels . . . |
| **James** | On the mountain . . . |
| **John** | And they told us, that one day, he will return. |
| **Peter** | Just the same way as we saw him go . . . |
| **Andrew** | One day . . . |
| **James** | He will come back. |
| **John** | And then, every knee shall bow . . . |
| **Thomas** | And every tongue confess . . . that Jesus Christ is Lord! |

# That's the Spirit

## (Pentecost Sunday)

### Introduction

This sketch uses an imagined meeting between Simon Peter and two police officers in Jerusalem to recount the events of the first Pentecost Sunday.

### Bible base

Acts 2. 1–42; Mark 14. 66–72

### Cast

Peter
Police Officer A
Police Officer B

*It is lunch-time on the day of Pentecost in Jerusalem. The two police officers are sitting behind a table. Peter is seated in front of them. He is full of energy and enthusiastic throughout, leaping up and down from time to time. There is a tape recorder on the table.*

| | |
|---|---|
| **Officer A** | *(Switching on the tape recorder)* |
| | Interview with one Simon Peter, Jerusalem, Day of Pentecost. |
| **Officer B** | *(To Peter)* You are Simon Peter? |
| **Peter** | Correct. |
| **Officer B** | From Galilee? |
| **Peter** | Correct again. |
| **Officer B** | Occupation? |
| **Peter** | Fisherman. Well, ex. Now I fish for men. |

| | |
|---|---|
| **Officer B** | (*To A*) What is he talking about? |
| **Officer A** | (*To B*) Look, don't expect to make sense of all this. Just ask the questions. |
| **Officer B** | All right. |
| | (*To Peter*) Well, sir, we've had a few complaints about disturbances in the city this morning. I should explain, you're not under arrest or anything. We just wanted to check up on what's going on. |
| **Officer A** | There are a lot of people out there who are a bit confused . . . |
| **Officer B** | Bewildered . . . |
| **Officer A** | Perplexed . . . |
| **Officer B** | Stunned . . . |
| **Peter** | (*Getting carried away*) |
| | Excited, amazed, challenged, thrilled? |
| **Officer B** | (*Grudgingly*) |
| | Well, yes. Some of them. Not all. We had some people in from Macedonia . . . |
| **Officer A** | Some from Cappadocia . . . |
| **Officer B** | Some from Pamphylia . . . |
| **Officer A** | Some from Egypt . . . |
| **Officer B** | Jews . . . |
| **Officer A** | Non-Jews . . . |
| **Officer B** | Cretans . . . |
| **Officer A** | Arabs . . . |
| **Peter** | Parthians, Medes, Elamites, Libyans . . . Never seen so many visitors in the city! What a fantastic opportunity! Today of all days! It's brilliant timing, isn't it? |
| **Officer A** | (*To B*) As I said, don't expect to make sense of all this. |
| **Officer B** | Well, the thing is, sir. All these foreign visitors said that when you and your lads started speaking this morning, |

**67**

|            | it was as though they were all hearing you talking in their own language. |
|------------|---|
| Peter      | Yes . . . |
| Officer B  | Well, it's a bit . . . spooky, isn't it? |
| Officer A  | A bit weird. |
| Officer B  | Perplexing. |
| Officer A  | Bewildering. |
| Peter      | (*Getting carried away again*) Miraculous! Amazing! Stunning! Exciting! |
| Officer B  | Yes, all right, sir. Just calm down, will you. |
| Officer A  | And then we've had these reports that when you spoke to the crowd, you claimed that the teacher Jesus of Nazareth . . . |
| Officer B  | . . . who we ourselves saw crucified, dead and buried, in this very city, only seven weeks ago . . . |
| Officer A  | . . . that he was alive again! Is this true? |
| Peter      | It certainly is! |
| Officer B  | What, true that you said it? |
| Peter      | Correct. |
| Officer B  | Or true that it happened? |
| Peter      | Correct again! |
| Officer B  | So, what exactly did you say about this Jesus that got them all so excited this morning? |
| Peter      | Well, I just reminded them first of all that they had seen and heard for themselves the miraculous things Jesus did and the amazing things he said. |
| Officer A  | Well, yes. That is true. We did see the signs. |
| Peter      | And that these all testified quite clearly that he was at least a man sent from God. |
| Officer B  | But he was arrested, and found guilty of something or other, I'm not sure what. |

| | |
|---|---|
| Peter | (*Getting more and more excited*) |
| | But that was all in God's purposes! All in his great plan of salvation! Your lot took him off and put him to death by nailing him on a cross. But then God raised him to life again, to prove that he was the Christ, the Son of the living God! Isn't that amazing? Isn't that stunning? Exciting? Miraculous! God has raised this Jesus to life! And me and all the others, well, we're witnesses to it! We've seen him. Spoken to him. Eaten with him. He's shown us how all his sufferings and now his raising again were all foretold in the scriptures! |
| | (*Now standing on his chair and speaking as though addressing a crowd*) |
| | Let all Israel be assured of this: God has made this Jesus, who you crucified, both Lord and Christ! |
| Officer A | Yes, all right, sir. Er, just calm down, will you. |
| Peter | (*Sitting down again*) |
| | Well, anyway, that's what I was telling them this morning. |
| Officer A | I see. Now, there is just one thing I don't quite get. |
| Officer B | (*To A*) Just one thing? |
| Officer A | (*To B*) Well, several actually. But let's try this one. |
| | (*To Peter*) Am I right in thinking, sir, that you are the same Simon Peter from Galilee that was overheard in Jerusalem on the morning before Passover denying three times that you even knew this Jesus of Nazareth? |
| Peter | Correct. |
| Officer B | And was later seen outside the temple courtyard crying like a three-year-old? |
| Peter | Correct again! |
| Officer A | Well, sir, how exactly do you explain it? The dramatic change, I mean. You don't appear to be the same person. What's happened to you that makes you stand up in the |

**69**

|  | city this morning in front of all those crowds, apparently without any fear or trepidation, and boldly claim that this Jesus has risen from the dead? |
|---|---|
| **Peter** | (*A little embarrassed*) Um. That's the Spirit . . . |
| **Officer B** | Spirit! Some of them said they thought you were drunk. We had you down for a few too many glasses of Chateau Bethany. But it's spirits, is it? |
| **Officer A** | And only nine o'clock in the morning. Tut, tut. Disgraceful. |
| **Peter** | No, what I meant was . . . |
| **Officer B** | (*Producing a 'breathalyser'*) I'm sorry, sir. But I shall have to ask you to breathe into this. |

(*Peter does so. The Officer examines it and is puzzled.*)

Mmm. Zero!

(*To A*) Steroids?

| **Peter** | Look, I'm not drunk! I'm not on drugs! |
|---|---|
|  | (*Getting excited again*) What's happened is simply what was foretold by the prophet Joel. God has poured out his Holy Spirit on us! |
| **Officer B** | Oh, the *Holy* Spirit! |

(*From this point on the two officers begin to be more sympathetic and interested.*)

| **Peter** | Yes! God has raised Jesus to life. Exalted to the right hand of God, Jesus has received from the Father the promised Holy Spirit and has poured him out on all of us who believe in him! That's what's happened to us this morning! |
|---|---|
| **Officer A** | Well, I suppose that *could* explain it all . . . |
| **Officer B** | But that would mean that Jesus . . . |
| **Officer A** | I know, but there has to be some explanation. Look, Simon Peter, maybe what you say is true . . . |
| **Officer B** | Maybe this Jesus of yours is risen from the dead . . . |
| **Officer A** | But if it is all true, what do we do? |

**Officer B**    Yes, tell us. What do we do?

**Peter**    (*Standing and opening his arms in invitation*)

Repent, and be baptised in the name of Jesus Christ for the forgiveness of your sins. And you too will receive the gift of the Holy Spirit! And this promise is not just for you – (*gesturing towards the audience*) but for all who the Lord our God will call, both here and far off, both now and in the years to come!

# THE GREAT ADVENTURE

*(Summer Holiday Club)*

## Introduction

This is a play in four episodes written for performance to children by adults or teenagers, as part of a holiday club, one episode per day. The play has been described as a cross between the Narnia stories, *Pilgrim's Progress* and the Famous Five! It was produced originally for a children's summer holiday club that we ran on the theme of 'Choices and Challenges'. As the characters make their way through their adventure they make various choices and face various challenges, all of which have parallels in the spiritual dimension of our lives. The play sets out to communicate such basic Christian ideas as the battle between good and evil, the idea that our selfishness and disobedience spoil God's good creation, and the message of the gospel, that God has sent his Son to bring us salvation, by giving his life for us and by conquering death and triumphing over evil. There is a challenge to the audience to follow the Lord Jesus and to choose the narrow path that leads to life. It is highly unlikely that the spiritual analogies will be transparent to a young audience, so it is essential that any performance of this play is supported by appropriate discussion and teaching.

## Cast

Silly Billy
Handy Mandy
Moany Tony
Cautious Cathy
the Maggie-Pie Bird
the Evil Nogard (a dragon)
Nilbog (a goblin)
the Stranger (also the King)

# Episode one

## Bible base

For example: Genesis 1–3 (Man's sin spoiling God's perfect creation); Acts 13. 32–33 (and other such references to Jesus as the one who was promised)

Silly Billy, Handy Mandy, Moany Tony, Cautious Cathy – the four adventurers – enter through the audience, creeping forward suspiciously, looking around nervously, consulting maps. There are several nervous jumps, with the characters scaring each other, and cries of 'Who's that? What's that?' and so on. On the stage is a closed door, standing all alone, to one side.

**Tony**        I don't like it here. I'm fed up. I wanna go home.

**Cathy**       Give it a rest, Tony.

**Mandy**       Always moaning, isn't he. Moany Tony, that's what we should call him.

**Billy**       I should let him go. He's ruining our adventure.

**Cathy**       Don't be silly, Billy. We're in this together.

**Tony**        Silly Billy!

**Mandy**       Come on everyone, let's not give up now. We've started, so we'll have to finish. No turning back. Right, Cathy?

**Cathy**       Er . . . right, Mandy.

(*They come across the door.*)

**Mandy**       Look at this.

**Billy**       It's a door!

**Tony**        (*Sarcastic*) No! Well done, Brain of Britain!

**Billy**       Do you think we should go through?

**Mandy**       I think we should give it a try.

**Cathy**       But we don't know what's on the other side! Let's not take any chances.

| | |
|---|---|
| Mandy | Don't be so cautious, Cathy. It might be better through there. |
| Tony | It might be worse. |
| Billy | It might be an outside toilet. |
| Cathy | Don't be silly, Billy! |
| Mandy | Well, I want to go through that door! |
| Tony | I wanna go home. |
| Mandy | Why don't we ring the bell? |
| Tony | It hasn't got one. |
| Billy | The man who made this door should have got the No-bell prize! |
| All | Don't be silly, Billy! |
| Mandy | Stand aside, I'm going to have a look. |
| | (*She tries to open the door, the handle comes off in her hand and she falls flat on her back, screaming, 'Ouch' etc.*) |
| Billy | That's handy, Mandy! (*Giggles*) Handy Mandy! |
| Cathy | Well, that's settled that! Now we can't go through the door. |
| Mandy | I'm sorry. |
| Tony | How disappointing. |

(*While they are talking, the Maggie-Pie Bird flies in and opens the door, but they don't notice it. The audience do, of course!*)

| | |
|---|---|
| Mandy | How can we get the door open? Have any of you got any good ideas? |
| Billy | Um! (*hopeful*) . . . no. |
| Cathy | Let's give it up. |
| Tony | Now that's a good idea. |
| Billy | I'm not giving up. |
| Mandy | (*Turning to the audience*) Has anyone got any good ideas? |

*(The audience, it is hoped, will call out, 'Behind you!' 'It's open!' and so on. After a bit of typical pantomime business the four adventurers turn round and are suitably surprised!)*

| | |
|---|---|
| **All** | *(To the Maggie-Pie Bird)* Who are you? |
| **Maggie-Pie** | I am the Maggie-Pie Bird! The messenger of the Great One. *(Indicating the open door)* The door to the kingdom of the Great One is open. You wish to go in? It is your choice. |
| **Mandy & Billy** | Yes please! |
| **Cathy** | Maybe . . . |
| **Tony** | I wanna go home. |
| **Maggie-Pie** | You may enter the kingdom of the Great One. There will be many good things for you to enjoy. But remember. The Great One commands that good things are to be shared. |

*(The Maggie-Pie Bird exits. The four walk one by one through the door, Mandy first, then Billy, then, cautiously, Cathy, and finally, very reluctantly, Tony. They look suitably delighted and fascinated as though discovering a new world. Improvise lots of 'Wow!' 'Look at that!' and so on.)*

| | |
|---|---|
| **Mandy** | This is . . . just perfect! |
| **Billy** | So peaceful. |
| **Cathy** | It's like . . . a new world! |

*(Tony lies down and stretches out as though sunbathing.)*

| | |
|---|---|
| **Tony** | This is great! |
| **Mandy** | Wanna go home now, Tony? |
| **Tony** | No thank you! This'll do fine! Wonderful sunshine! |
| **Billy** | Move over, I'll join you. Remember, good things are to be shared. |
| | *(Billy also stretches out and sunbathes.)* |
| **Cathy** | Careful, you'll get sunburn. |
| | *(She puts a huge dollop of suntan lotion on Tony's nose.)* |

There, we don't want you looking like Rudolf the red-nosed reindeer.

**Billy**   Did you say rain, dear? But there isn't a cloud in the sky!

**All**   Don't be silly Billy!

**Tony**   I think I could be really happy here.

**Billy**   All good friends together.

**Mandy**   Come on, cautious Cathy, let's explore some more.

(*Mandy and Cathy go off to various parts exploring. Separately, Mandy discovers a Marshmallow-Tree and enjoys herself eating some of the marshmallows, while Cathy finds a Pepsi-Cola Stream and has a good drink. Improvise appropriate dialogue for these discoveries. Cathy then wanders over and bumps into Mandy who is just finishing off a marshmallow.*)

**Cathy**   What're you eating?

**Mandy**   Oh, er, nothing. So, what did you find over there?

**Cathy**   Oh, er, nothing specially interesting.

**Mandy**   ʾ Same over here.

**Cathy**   You sure you're not eating something.

**Mandy**   Come on. Let's get back to the others.

(*They return to the other two and join them in their sunbathing. There's lots of pushing and cries of 'Move over!' and so on. Gradually an argument develops between the four of them. Then suddenly they start to feel cold and sit up, shivering.*)

**Tony**   I'm cold!

**Cathy**   So am I!

**Mandy**   Look! There's a terrible storm coming up.

**Billy**   All the leaves are coming off the trees!

**Mandy**   (*Covering her ears*) What's that terrifying noise?

**Cathy**   (*Shielding her eyes*) And that blinding light?

**Tony**   I'm scared!

**Mandy**   Something's gone wrong!

**Billy**   What's happening?

| Cathy | It's all ruined! |
|---|---|
| Tony | I wanna go home! |

(*The Maggie-Pie Bird returns dramatically and points them to the door.*)

**Maggie-Pie** You have disobeyed the command of the Great One and brought evil into his kingdom. Now you must leave this place and go on your journey. One day you may return, but first you must make many choices and face many challenges. The Great One gives you this message. 'On your journey, look for . . . the One who is Promised! Find him and you may return. But first the evil Nogard must be defeated.' Now go!

(*Sheepishly, the four leave through the door. Maggie-Pie slams it shut behind them and exits.*)

| Billy | What do we do now? |
|---|---|
| Tony | I wanna go home. |
| Mandy | Well, you can't. Just stop moaning. |
| Tony | Well, it's not my fault we're in this mess. |
| Billy | Moany Tony! |
| Cathy | Look, stop arguing. We've got to get going on our journey. |
| Mandy | We've been such fools, haven't we. Through there, we had a glimpse of the kingdom of the Great One. But we spoilt it with our selfishness. |
| Billy | And our arguing. |
| Tony | And now we're lost. |
| Cathy | It's hopeless. |
| Mandy | Not completely hopeless. Not if we can find . . . the One who is Promised! |

(*All exit.*)

# Episode two

## Bible base

For example:  Matthew 6. 23 and 7. 7 (seeking God's kingdom);
Psalm 119. 105 (God's word a light for our path);
Luke 19. 10 (Jesus came to seek the lost)

*The stage is completely clear. The four adventurers enter.*

**Cathy**   Where do you think we are, Mandy?

**Mandy**   Well, I would say, that we are roughly, just about, in a word, lost.

**Tony**   Well, it's not my fault. I didn't want to come on this adventure in the first place!

**Billy**   He doesn't get any better, does he? Moany Tony!

**Cathy**   Look, we mustn't squabble, or we'll never work out how to get back to the kingdom of the Great One.

**Mandy**   Remember what he said: look for the One who is Promised and you may return . . .

**Billy**   . . . but first the evil Nogard must be defeated! Nogard. Sounds horrible. I'm scared!

**Tony**   (*Creeping up behind him*)

I am the evil Nogard! (*Roars*)

(*Billy reacts appropriately.*)

**Billy**   Stop that, Tony! This is scary enough as it is!

**Mandy**   (*Looking at a map*)

Right, I think I've got the route worked out. Follow me. Down this path here. Head for that weird-looking tree. I'm sure this is right. Ah, a fork. Now, let's see, left or right?

(*Improvise a journey around the hall, including clambering through the audience, who can be referred to variously as a smelly swamp, ugly-looking bushes, poisonous snakes, and so on. The other three follow Mandy, but keep asking, 'Is this right?*

*Are you sure?' and so on. Eventually they get back on to the stage.)*

**Tony**      Congratulations, Mandy.

**Mandy**    Congratulations?

**Tony**      Yes, congratulations, you've taken us on this long, difficult journey, and succeeded in leading us right back to where we were three hours ago!

**Mandy**    Oh, yes. Sorry!

**Cathy**     I'm sure it's no good just going our own way. We've got to find the way that the Great One wants us to follow.

*(Billy has sat down and adopted a meditating pose.)*

**Tony**      What're you doing? You look silly, Billy!

**Billy**      I'm concentrating.

**Mandy**    On what?

**Billy**      Well, I thought if I concentrated really hard I might get some inspiration as to which way to go.

**Cathy**     Good idea! Let's all do it!

*(They all sit and meditate, visibly concentrating hard, one in each of the four corners of the stage. Suddenly, all together they shout 'Got it!' In unison, they leap up and all point in the direction of centre stage, shouting 'That way!' They charge forward and all collide, collapsing in a heap.)*

**Cathy**     It's hopeless!

**Mandy**    We're lost for ever.

**Tony**      I wanna go home.

**Billy**      Wait a bit! I've got another idea . . .

              *(Very feebly)*  Help! Help!

              *(Stronger)*  Help!

*(The others join in, gradually increasing the volume. They decide it's not loud enough and get the audience to join in. Eventually . . .)*

**Mandy**    Stop! Quiet! Listen! What's that?

*(Outside we hear Nilbog singing 'Somewhere over the Rainbow'. He enters.)*

**Mandy**    Who are you?

| | |
|---|---|
| **Tony** | It's Noddy. |
| **Cathy** | Can you help us? |
| **Billy** | Why are you wearing your pyjamas? |
| **Nilbog** | I am Nilbog, the goblin. Actually I am a hippopotamus. I should warn you that if I say something that is true the next thing I say will be untrue. I just told you a lie. |
| **Mandy** | I get it. So you are a goblin, but you're not a hippopotamus! |
| **Nilbog** | You are correct. I am a hippopotamus. |
| **Billy** | Are you a friendly goblin? |
| **Nilbog** | Yes, I am really friendly. And I hate people like you. I didn't mean that, of course. And I didn't mean that either. |
| **Tony** | I'm getting confused. |
| **Cathy** | Excuse me, Mr Nilbog, but can you help us find the one who is promised, the one who will show us the way back to the kingdom of the Great One? |
| **Nilbog** | Of course, I can. I haven't the faintest idea what you are talking about. Now, listen carefully and I will direct you to someone who will give you a choice. If you make the right choice you will go wrong. |
| **Mandy** | Wait a moment, I'll write this down. (*She writes on a pad*) |
| **Nilbog** | Down the steps. Turn right at the cross-roads. Forward ten paces. Turn left. Cross the rocks ahead of you. Don't go through the tunnel. Climb up the hill ahead of you. Stand on your heads. Shout as loud as you can, 'Oojie-squoojie-fizzly-wizz.' And no-one will come to help you. Good-bye for now. Have a horrible day. (*Exit*) |
| **Mandy** | (*With the others joining in, ad lib*) |
| | So, what do we do? Down the steps. Right? That's true. |
| | (*They go off the stage into the auditorium and act out the instructions appropriately.*) |
| | Turn right at the cross-roads. That must be false, so that means we have to . . . |

(*Consulting the audience at each stage to decide what to do . . .*)

. . . turn left! Forward ten paces. That must be true . . . Turn left. That must be false, so we . . . turn right. Cross the rocks ahead of you. True. Don't go through the tunnel. False, so we . . . do go through the tunnel. Climb up the hill ahead of you. True.

(*Back on to the stage*)

Stand on your heads. False, thank goodness! Shout as loud as you can, 'Oojie-squoojie-fizzly-wizz.' Do we do that? Yes!

(*They all shout, with the audience joining in.*)

And no-one will come to help you. So that means . . . someone will come to help us!

**Cathy**     Listen, someone's coming!

(*Off-stage we hear Nilbog singing again.*)

**Billy**     Is it the one who is promised?

**Nilbog**     (*Enters, carrying a sack*) No, it's me, Nilbog! Oh, no, it isn't.

**Tony**     Don't start that again.

**Nilbog**     You have done very well to follow my directions. You are all very stupid. Now you must choose something that you might need on your journey.

**Tony**     I'm confused. Is this the truth?

**Nilbog**     No, it's a lie.

**Cathy**     I think that means it's true.

**Nilbog**     You may choose a torch or a bag of money. But it doesn't matter what you choose.

**Billy**     That means it does matter!

(*As they make their choices, Nilbog hands over a torch or a bag of money, as appropriate.*)

**Mandy**     If it will help me to find my way to the One who is Promised, I'll have a torch.

**Billy**     I'll do the same as Mandy.

| | |
|---|---|
| **Tony** | Don't be silly, Billy. Take the money! It will bring you great happiness, won't it? |
| **Billy** | I don't think that's what he really meant . . . No, I'm not silly. I'll take a torch. |
| **Tony** | What about you, Cathy? |
| **Cathy** | Um, I'm not sure . . . Oh, I'll have a torch as well. |
| **Tony** | Well, I'll have the money, thanks. |
| **Nilbog** | You three have chosen wisely. But Tony has made the wisest choice. (*Laughs*) |
| | Good-bye. Have a horrible day. And, remember, beware of the evil Nogard! He's absolutely harmless! (*Exit*) |

# Episode three

## Bible base

*For example: Matthew 6. 24 (cannot serve both God and money); Matthew 7. 13–14 (the broad and narrow roads); John 14. 6 (Jesus, the way to the Father); Matthew 28. 20 (Jesus's promise to be with us always)*


*On the stage there is a sign-post pointing two ways, indicating 'The Broad Path' and 'The Narrow Path'. The Maggie-Pie Bird enters.*

**Maggie-Pie**    I am the Maggie-Pie Bird, the messenger of the Great One. The story so far. Silly Billy, Handy Mandy, Moany Tony and Cautious Cathy are on a great adventure. They found a door, went in and had a glimpse of the wonderful kingdom of the Great One. But they had to leave because they did not obey his command and they spoilt his perfect world with their selfishness and arguing. They have been told they might one day return, but first they must look for the One who is Promised. So far all they have done is to go round in circles and to bump into Nilbog the Goblin. He offered them a choice: a torch or some money. Three of them chose a torch, but Tony chose the moany. Sorry, the money. Now they continue on their journey. But they must remember to . . . beware the evil Nogard! Look here they come. I will hide and observe their progress . . .

*(She hides. The four enter through the audience again. Tony is lagging behind. Improvise leaping over crevasses, climbing cliffs, battling through the undergrowth, swimming through raging torrents.)*

**Mandy**    I'm glad we've got these torches. We'd never see the path in this dark forest without them.

**Cathy**    *(Calling him)* Come on, Tony. Keep up!

**Billy**    What is he doing?

**Mandy**    Counting his money again, I think.

| | |
|---|---|
| Tony | Ninety-eight, ninety-nine, a hundred. A hundred pounds. Wow! Here, you lot, wait for me! (*He rushes to catch up.*) |
| Cathy | If you keep stopping to count your money, you'll get lost, you know. |
| Tony | You sure this is the right road? I don't think it can be. Look at that tree. I'm sure we've been here before. I wish I was at home. |
| Billy | Don't be so moany, Tony. If only we can find the One who is Promised we'll be able to get back to the kingdom of the Great One. Don't you remember how wonderful it was there? |
| Tony | S'pose so. |
| Mandy | Look ahead of us, there's a fork in the road. |

(*Billy rushes ahead and picks up a fork!*)

| | |
|---|---|
| Billy | What, this fork? |
| Cathy | Don't be silly, Billy. |

(*They all come up to the sign-post and are clearly puzzled. They discuss which way they should go: ad lib this.*)

| | |
|---|---|
| Billy | If only there was someone to help us make our choice. |
| Mandy | Like that nice Mr Nilbog. |
| Tony | Oh no, not him. He just confused me. |
| Cathy | Or that Maggie-Pie Bird. She knew what was what. But I don't suppose we'll ever see her again. |
| Billy | No. We've said good-bye to her for ever, I should think. |

(*The Maggie-Pie Bird waves from behind her hiding-place. They don't see her, but the audience do. Between them the four adventurers interact with the audience and get them involved in drawing their attention to her. Some typical pantomime business: 'Where?' 'Behind you!' Eventually they see her and react appropriately.*)

| | |
|---|---|
| Billy | It's you! |
| Mandy | We thought we'd never see you again! |

*(The stranger enters quietly and sits unobtrusively on one corner of the stage, watching and listening.)*

**Maggie-Pie**    You see there is always help somewhere if you look for it. Now what do you want to know?

**All**    Which way to go!

**Maggie-Pie**    Can you not read the sign-posts? This way is the broad path. And that way is the narrow path.

**Tony**    Thank you very much. That's a great help!

**Maggie-Pie**    Ah, I sense from your tone, Tone, that you do not know how to choose.

**Tony**    Well . . .

**Maggie-Pie**    A choice must be made. Choose wisely, my friends. But it is not for me to guide you. Farewell. Look for the promised one. Beware the evil Nogard! *(Exit)*

*(The four are still puzzled about which way to go. Billy sees the stranger.)*

**Billy**    Look over there. That bloke with the walking-stick. Do you think he might be able to help us?

**Tony**    Shouldn't think so. No-one seems much help around here.

**Mandy**    We've got nothing to lose.

**Cathy**    Excuse me, sir!

**Stranger**    Yes, Cathy? What is it?

**Cathy**    How did he know my name?

**Mandy**    Look, sir, we've got to choose one of these two ways to go. Do you know what they're like?

**Stranger**    I think I have some idea. I've been most places in my time.

*(Standing up and going across to the sign-post)*

On the left you have the broad path. Some people say that's the one that leads to the bright lights. Very popular that path. Lots of people go that way. You'll find plenty of things to spend your money on. Nice and

**85**

broad, easy-going. You can take that road if you like. But you won't find your way back to the kingdom of the Great One, I'm afraid. For that, you will have to take the narrow path. It's hard work, I warn you. Steep, dangerous, and dark at times. You'll need to be brave and strong-hearted. Not many people choose to go that way.

**Cathy**        And which way are you heading, sir?

**Stranger**     The narrow way. Will you . . . follow me?

**Billy**        And if we go this way, will we avoid the evil Nogard?

**Stranger**     I cannot promise that. It seems he is everywhere at times.

**Mandy**        And the One who is Promised?

**Stranger**     He will be there, along the narrow path. That is why he is promised – to see you safely through. Trust me.

**Mandy**        What do you think, Cathy? Billy? Tony? Should we trust him?

**Cathy**        Maybe . . .

**Billy**        Of course we should. Don't you see . . . it must be . . .

**Tony**         Well, I'm not going to trust him. Look at him. A scruffy old tramp. Anyway, I don't want to go anywhere dark again. I'm going for the bright lights. I've had enough of looking for the kingdom of the Great One. I'm going this way.

                 (*He starts to go in the direction of the broad path*)

**Billy**        Tony, stop! Don't you see? The One who is Promised . . . he'll be with us on the path, if we go this way . . .

**Tony**         Anyone with me? Look I've got plenty of money. We'll be OK this way.

**Cathy**        Yeah, I'll come with you, Tony. I'm not sure I ever believed in this One who is Promised, anyway! Here, you can have this, I won't be needing it.

                 (*She gives her torch to the Stranger*)

**Stranger**     Good-bye, Cathy. Good-bye, Tony. We will not meet again. We go our separate ways.

**Tony**          I can live with that. Good-bye all.

**Cathy**         'Bye everyone.

*(Cathy and Tony set off. The other two wave good-bye, sadly.)*

I'm still puzzled as to how he knew my name. Oh well, never mind. Let's get going.

*(They exit, whistling merrily.)*

**Mandy**         Now there's just the two of us.

**Billy**          *(Indicating the Stranger)* Three.

**Stranger**      Now a dangerous journey lies ahead of us. You will need these cloaks to protect you.

*(He takes from his bag two cloaks and gives them to Mandy and Billy.)*

And these swords to defend yourselves.

*(He looks behind the sign-post and finds two swords for them.)*

Come, we must get started.

*(They set off. They come soon to what appears to be a dangerous ridge to cross. Ad lib this. The Stranger goes first and helps them across to safety. Then suddenly, just as they get to the end of the ridge, there are screams off-stage. Tony and Cathy come running in, pursued by the dragon, Nogard, who is roaring ferociously. They charge round the hall, with the two of them shouting 'It's Nogard! It's Nogard! Help!' and so on, then exit. There are more screams off-stage.)*

**Mandy**         Did you hear that noise . . . What was it?

**Billy**          I don't know. But it seemed a long way off.

*(They look around.)*

**Stranger**      Keep your eyes straight ahead. Do not look either to the left or to the right. Just follow me.

*(They exit.)*

# Episode four

## Bible base

*For example: 1 Peter 5. 8 and Ephesians 6. 10–18 (spiritual warfare and spiritual armour); 1 Peter 3.18 (and other such references to Christ's death for us, to bring us to God); Colossians 2. 15 and 1 John 4. 4 (Christ's victory over the forces of evil)*

*The door is in place on the stage, closed. There is a plank leading from, e.g., a table off-stage, across to the stage. To begin with all the action takes place off the stage, in the auditorium. The stage directions throughout, especially for the final battle between Nogard and the Stranger, will clearly have to be adapted to the circumstances in which the play is performed. Nogard enters and is very fierce.*

Nogard      (*Roars*)

I am the evil Nogard. I am a nasty, fire-breathing, man-eating dragon. I'm really horrible, especially on Fridays (*name the actual day*). I'm so terrifying I even frighten myself.

(*Roars*)

Oooh, I really scared myself that time. So there are just two of these adventurers left. And that man with them. He's a nuisance, always turning up to help people. But this time I shall show him. They'll not get past me. I've eaten a hundred garlic onions this morning and my breath can destroy anyone! Aaaah! Aaaah!

(*Lots of roaring and so on. He hides.*)

(*Enter Billy and Mandy, following the Stranger. Improvise getting over various hazards. Then they come to an imaginary dead-end.*)

Stranger      Now, my two friends, Billy and Mandy. We must get to that rock over there (*pointing to the table with the plank*), but the path has collapsed. We have a choice. We take the high route along that steep and dangerous crag (*pointing along the front of the stage*). Or we turn back.

| | |
|---|---|
| **Billy** | What are you going to do? |
| **Stranger** | If you will trust me and go on, I will go with you. |
| **Mandy** | We'll trust you all right! |
| **Stranger** | You have made the right choice. Follow me. |

(*Improvise, climbing on to the edge of the stage and working their way along, as though along a narrow crag, with the Stranger leading and helping. They get across. Then suddenly Nogard leaps out at them. They react appropriately. Ad lib action and dialogue, including . . .*)

| | |
|---|---|
| **Billy** | Help! What's that? |
| **Mandy** | It must be . . . Nogard! |
| **Billy** | The flames coming from his mouth! We'll be burnt to a cinder! |
| **Stranger** | Trust me! I promised I would be with you and see you through! |
| **Mandy** | The Promised One! It's you! |
| **Billy** | That's right! Didn't you realise? |
| **Nogard** | You will not pass! I shall have you all grilled for my breakfast! |
| **Stranger** | Oh no you won't! Your cloaks! Billy, Mandy! Put on your cloaks. They will protect you from the flames! |
| | (*Pointing to the door*) Now, look, the door is ahead of you. |
| | (*He advances towards Nogard who strikes him. He falls.*) |
| **Stranger** | (*Calling out to Billy and Mandy*) Run for your lives! |

(*They run. Nogard pursues them. They stumble.*)

| | |
|---|---|
| **Stranger** | (*Still on the ground, calling*) Your swords! Use your swords! Defend yourselves. I'm coming! |

(*They hold off Nogard for a while, but are losing . . . The Stranger gets up and gets there just in time . . .. He takes a sword and fights Nogard.*)

| | |
|---|---|
| **Stranger** | I'll take care of Nogard! You two . . . go . . . Look, the door is there. Get to the door . . . get across the ravine to safety. Go! Go now! Leave the battle to me. Trust me! |

*(He holds off Nogard with the sword. Billy and Mandy get to safety across the plank and collapse in front of the door. Nogard gradually drives the Stranger back until they are both up on the plank. The sword is dropped, they wrestle and fall into the imaginary deep ravine! They roll off together out of sight, off-stage. Billy and Mandy react appropriately. They cry out in despair. There is silence. Then the Maggie-Pie Bird enters and opens the door.)*

**Maggie-Pie**    The door is now open for you. Come, enter the kingdom of the Great One.

**Billy**    But . . . the One who was Promised . . .

**Maggie-Pie**    His work there is finished. He has defeated the evil Nogard. You are safe now.

**Mandy**    It was him all the time!

**Billy**    May we really come in? And stay?

**Maggie-Pie**    That is his purpose for you. If you had not disobeyed you could have stayed last time and all this *(pointing to the ravine)* . . . all that . . . *(sadly)* would not have been necessary.

**Mandy**    We're really sorry.

**Billy**    You mean, it was our fault that . . .

**Maggie-Pie**    Now you understand? But come, a feast is prepared. But first there is for you something very special. The Great One himself wishes to speak with you. Look, he comes now. Fall to your knees!

*(They do so, with bowed heads. The Stranger, now dressed as a King, comes up on to the stage and stands in front of them.)*

**King**    Now, my two friends, Billy and Mandy. Welcome to my kingdom!

**Mandy**    It's you!

**Billy**    You're not dead! You're . . . alive!

**King**    *(He puts his arms around them and leads them through the door)*

    Come, let us celebrate. The battle is won. Your journey is over. You are safe in my kingdom!

# The rich fool

*(Harvest)*

## Introduction

This sketch combines the parable of the rich fool with the teaching on not worrying unduly about material things, which follows the parable in Luke's Gospel.

## Bible base

*Luke 12. 13–34*

## Cast

Rich Man (Mr Robinson)
Secretary (Tracy)
Narrators 1 and 2
Raven, Messenger

*The Rich Man is seated at his desk, with all the trappings of a successful business-man. His secretary, Tracy, sits with notepad and pencil poised. They are stationary during the introduction. The two Narrators enter and deliver their lines in an exaggeratedly serious manner, with lots of emphasis.*

**Narrator 1**    Ladies and gentlemen.

**Narrator 2**    Girls and boys.

**Narrator 1**    Look out!

**Narrator 2**    Be warned!

**Narrator 1**    Be on your guard . . .

**Narrator 2**    . . . against . . .

**Narrator 1**    . . . against all kinds of greed.

**Narrator 2**    And remember!

| | |
|---|---|
| **Narrator 1** | Remember this! |
| **Narrator 2** | Don't forget it! |
| **Narrator 1** | Um . . . er . . . |
| | (*To Narrator 2, in a whisper*) What do we have to remember? |
| **Narrator 2** | (*Whispering back*) I forget. Wait a bit. I'll look it up. |
| | (*Gets out a pocket Bible and searches through it*) |
| | Um, Luke 12, verse 15 . . . (*Reading*) 'You're out of your mind.' |
| **Narrator 1** | What? |
| **Narrator 2** | Oh, sorry. That's Acts 12, verse 15. |
| | (*Turning over pages*) Wait, wait, wait. Here it is . . . |
| **Narrator 1** | So, remember this . . . |
| **Narrator 2** | (*Reading*) ' . . . a person's life does not consist in the abundance of their possessions.' |

(*The Rich Man and Secretary come to life.*)

| | |
|---|---|
| **Rich Man** | (*To Narrator 2*) You're out of your mind. |
| **Narrator 1** | (*Pointing*) Rich man. |
| **Secretary** | Yes, Mr Robinson. |
| **Narrator 2** | (*Pointing*) Secretary. |
| **Rich man** | (*To secretary*) Take a message, Tracy. |
| **Narrator 1** | (*With a sweep of the hand towards Rich Man and Secretary*) |
| | Parable. |

(*The two Narrators step back now.*)

| | |
|---|---|
| **Secretary** | Yes, Mr Robinson. |
| **Rich Man** | To my finance manager. Message reads. 'Reduce investments in building society shares. Re-invest large quantities of capital in personal insurance.' |
| **Secretary** | (*Making notes*) All done, Mr Robinson. |
| **Rich Man** | Pass me that report on my farming developments. |

| | |
|---|---|
| Secretary | (*Passing over a document*) There you are, Mr Robinson. |
| Rich Man | (*Looking through the document*) Excellent. Huge EC subsidies again. Vast crop output. Gigantic profits next year. Take a message, Tracy. |
| Secretary | Yes, Mr Robinson. |
| Rich Man | To my estate manager. Message reads. 'Replace all small storage units with new mega-sized storage units immediately.' |
| Secretary | (*Making notes*) All done, Mr Robinson. |
| Rich Man | Now make me an appointment for Monday morning with my bank manager, fix up a session with my therapist on Monday afternoon, book a table for four on Tuesday evening at the usual expensive restaurant, book me a flight to Brussels for Wednesday afternoon, call a meeting of the board for Thursday when I return, and telephone my wife to say I'll be late home tonight, dinner at 9 o'clock and to make sure my dinner jacket and dress shirt are ready for the Brussels trip. |
| Secretary | Right away, Mr Robinson. No problem, Mr Robinson. |
| | (*Exit*) |
| Rich Man | Now, where's my memo-pad? (*Calling*) Tracy, do you keep stationery in your office? |
| Secretary | (*From off-stage*) No, sometimes I move around a bit. |
| Rich Man | Well, get me a new memo-pad. Right away. |
| Secretary | (*From off-stage*) Right away, Mr Robinson! |

(*A note-pad comes flying through the air from off-stage aimed at Mr Robinson's desk.*)

| | |
|---|---|
| Rich Man | Thank you! |
| | (*Talking to himself as he shifts piles of paper round*) |
| | Now, better work my way through this lot. Let's see. Financial summaries for all my investments. Channel Island bank account statement. |
| | (*He starts to appear visibly tired, yawning and so on*) |

Budget forecasts for next year. Cash flow estimates. New regulations for EC farming subsidies.

(*Picking up a memo, but only just able to keep his eyes open with tiredness*)

And what's this?

(*Big yawn, then reading*) 'Telephone message from Mrs Robinson. Don't forget to write your will before flying to Brussels.'

(*He drifts off to sleep*) Don't forget . . . to write your will . . .

(*He slumps forward on to his desk, asleep. He is now dreaming.*)

| | |
|---|---|
| Narrator 1 | (*As a TV announcer*) And now on BBC1 it's time for the nine o'clock news. |
| Narrator 2 | (*As a BBC news reader*)  Good evening. Here is the news at nine o'clock, for Wednesday the twentieth of October. Reports are coming in of a serious plane crash over Belgium. As yet we have no definite news of any survivors . . . |

(*The Rich Man wakes with a start and is visibly shaken, then relieved to realise he was only dreaming.*)

| | |
|---|---|
| Rich Man | Oh, golly! Oh. I must have been dreaming. |

(*He begins to drift off to sleep again*)

Must remember . . . write my will . . . check travel insurance . . . mortgage protection policy . . .

(*He is now asleep. He is dreaming again. Someone dressed as a raven enters. The Narrators step forward for their lines, then retreat again.*)

| | |
|---|---|
| Narrator 1 | Is he dreaming again? |
| Narrator 2 | That's right. But this time he's talking to the birds. |
| Rich Man | (*He sits upright and speaks to the raven*) What are you doing in my dream? |
| Raven | (*In a messenger-of-doom voice*) I am a messenger, sent to warn you. |
| Rich Man | So, who do you work for? |

Raven            I do not work, for anyone. I am a raven.

*(Suddenly changing from serious voice)* Can't you tell?

*(Back to serious)* I do not sow. I do not reap. I have no storerooms or barns. Yet I never go hungry. For God feeds me, as he feeds all the birds of the air. And you, Mr Robinson? Why do you worry so much about your financial security and your personal investments? Do you think that by worrying you can add a single hour to your life? Don't be a fool, Mr Robinson. *(Starts to exit)* Don't be a fool. Remember the ravens . . .

*(The raven exits. Enter a messenger carrying a bunch of flowers.)*

Messenger        Flowers for Mr Robinson.

Rich Man         Flowers for me? Why has someone sent me flowers?

Messenger        Could be one of a number of reasons, Mr Robinson. You know the kind of thing, birthdays, anniversaries, deaths . . . oh, sorry to mention death again. But, then, when all is said and done, it comes to us all in the end.

*(The Messenger hands over the flowers.)*

Rich Man         *(Looking wistfully at the flowers)* They're . . . very lovely.

Messenger        Oh, yes, there was a message with them. Let's see.

*(Reading)* 'Just look at these flowers. Beautiful, or what? Yet they don't have to work hard to buy expensive clothes to look as splendid as this. God clothes them in their own special beauty. And they're only flowers, here today, gone tomorrow.'

*(Messenger starts to exit)*

Think about it, Mr Robinson. Think about it. Remember the flowers of the field . . .

*(The Messenger exits. The Rich Man falls asleep again, leaving the flowers on the desk. The Secretary enters, picks up the flowers and arranges them in a vase.)*

Secretary        There you are, Mr Robinson. A nice bunch of flowers to cheer the office up. Mr Robinson! Wake up now, Mr Robinson, it's nearly time for your next appointment.

*(She gives him a gentle shake)* Mr Robinson . . .

**Rich Man**  *(He wakes up)* Oh dear. Oh. I was . . . dreaming . . .

*(He sees the flowers)*  Those flowers? Where did they come from?

**Secretary**  I just thought they'd cheer the office up, Mr Robinson. Just a few flowers. But, but if you don't like them . . .

**Rich Man**  Oh, no, no. That's fine. They're . . . um, lovely. Thanks.

**Secretary**  *(Pointing as though at the office window)* Oh, look! There's a bird sitting on the window ledge.

**Rich Man**  *(Burying his head in his hands)* Oh no. Don't tell me. It's not a raven, is it?

**Secretary**  No, it's a sparrow. Silly Mr Robinson. A raven!

**Rich Man**  *(Leaping into action)* Right. Take a message, Tracy. To myself. Message reads. 'Stop being a fool, Mr Robinson. As from today. Reduce personal investment in material things with immediate effect. Re-invest large quantities of time, energy and personal resources in eternal things. Open up new bank account in heaven. Aim to accumulate treasure there and stop worrying about treasure on earth.' End of message.

**Narrators**  Beginning of life.

# Family reunion

## (Harvest)

## Introduction

This is a perfectly straightforward dramatised version of the wonderful Biblical account of Joseph's reunion with his brothers, as, prompted by the famine, they travelled to Egypt in search of food for their family in Canaan. Its relevance to harvest is simply that Joseph was able to help both the people of his adopted country and his own family during the times of shortage, because of the wisdom that he had shown in managing the surplus during the times of plenty. The story of Joseph's meeting with the brothers who had sold him into slavery and his testing of their motives is told with such dramatic impact in the Bible itself that it requires little more than simple retelling. Only a few stage directions are included in the script. Appropriate action is assumed throughout in accordance with the dialogue and the extent of the acting element decided for the production. The script can be delivered as not much more than a dramatised reading with minimal action and props, or in full biblical costume with all the props implied by the story, such as sacks of corn and bags of gold. Given the length and structure of this piece, it might be appropriate, for example in the context of a church service, to present it in three or four parts separated by songs and prayers.

## Bible base

*Genesis 42–45*

## Cast

Jacob
Reuben
Judah
Simeon
Benjamin

Joseph
Steward
Egyptian Guard (non-speaking part)
Up to seven other brothers (non-speaking parts) may be included as
well.

*One side of the acting area represents Canaan, the other side Egypt, as far apart
as possible. The various characters travel backwards and forwards between
'Canaan' and 'Egypt', so a clearly-defined 'route' across the acting area is required.
Jacob, Benjamin, Reuben, Judah and Simeon (and any other brothers taking part)
are together in 'Canaan'. Joseph is seated in 'Egypt'. The steward and the guard
stand beside him.)*

**Reuben**    *(To Jacob)* Father Jacob, the famine here in Canaan is severe.
Our families are starving.

**Jacob**    I have heard there is corn in Egypt, Reuben *(pointing generally
in the direction of Egypt)*. Go down there and buy some for us,
so that we may live and not die.

*(Gesturing to the other sons)* You others go as well. But leave
Benjamin, my youngest son, here with me, lest any harm
come to him.

*(All the brothers except Benjamin pack up, make their farewells and travel across
the divide between 'Canaan' and 'Egypt'. They arrive in Egypt and are met by the
steward. He goes across to Joseph.)*

**Steward**    Joseph, governor of Egypt. Some men are here to buy corn.

*(Joseph turns to face the visitors and is taken aback to see who they are. He makes
an aside to the audience.)*

**Joseph**    I cannot believe this. These are my brothers! After so many
years!

*(To the brothers, harshly)* Where do you come from?

**Judah**    From the land of Canaan, my lord, to buy food.

**Joseph**    *(Aside)* So, they do not recognise me.

*(To the brothers)* You are spies! You have come to find out
where our land is unprotected!

| | |
|---|---|
| **Reuben** | No, my lord. Your servants have come to buy food. We are all the sons of one man. We are honest men, not spies. |
| **Joseph** | No! I do not believe you. You are spies. |
| **Simeon** | Sir, this is not so. We are – we were – twelve brothers, the sons of one man, Jacob by name, who lives in the land of Canaan. The youngest is now with our father. And one is no more. |
| **Joseph** | Is that so? Well, I say you are spies. And this is how you will be tested. As surely as Pharaoh lives, you will not leave this place until this youngest brother of whom you speak comes here. Until then you will be kept in prison. |
| **Reuben** | Have mercy on us, my lord. |
| **Joseph** | Lock them up! |

*(The guard escorts the brothers off-stage. Joseph and the steward follow after them.)*

*(The steward enters and holds up a card saying 'three days later'. Joseph enters and takes his seat. The guard ushers in the brothers.)*

| | |
|---|---|
| **Joseph** | During the three days you have been here, I have given some thought to your case. I have decided that one of you shall stay here in prison, while the rest of you go back with corn for your starving households. But you must bring your youngest brother to me, so that your story may be verified, and so that you may not die. |
| **Simeon** | *(To his brothers)* Surely we are being punished because of what we did to our brother Joseph. |
| **Reuben** | Didn't I tell you, Simeon, not to sin against the boy? But you would not listen. Now we are to pay for what we did to him. |
| **Joseph** | *(Pointing to Simeon)* Take this one away and bind him securely. |

*(The guard takes Simeon out. Joseph speaks to the steward.)*

Fill their bags with grain.

*(In confidence, to his steward)* And put the silver that each man has paid for the grain back in their sacks.

*(Appropriate action. Then the brothers, without Simeon, set off for Canaan. Halfway along the route they stop and act appropriately to the following dialogue)*

**Judah**   Brothers, look. I opened my sack to get some grain to feed my donkey and my silver has been returned! Here it is in my sack!

(*They are all aghast! Each brother looks in his sack and reacts appropriately as he discovers that his silver is returned as well.*)

**Reuben**   And mine too! What is this that God has done to us? Come, let us return quickly to our father.

(*Appropriate action. They arrive in Canaan and are greeted by Jacob.*)

**Jacob**   What news, my sons? Do you bring us grain from Egypt, Reuben? Did it go well, Judah?

**Reuben**   It is bad news, father. The man who is lord over all the land of Egypt spoke harshly to us and treated us as though we were spies.

**Judah**   Simeon is taken prisoner and we must return with our youngest brother Benjamin to prove that we are honest men. Only then will he return Simeon to us and allow us to trade in the land of Egypt.

**Reuben**   And, look, it is worse. In each of our sacks we find the pouch of silver we paid for the grain. Surely this man plots to bring trouble upon us.

**Jacob**   Oh, great is my misery! You have deprived me of my children. Joseph is no more. Simeon is taken from me. And now you want to take Benjamin. Everything is against me!

**Reuben**   Entrust him to my care, father. I promise to bring him back to you. My own two sons will be your hostages to make sure I keep my word.

**Jacob**   No, Benjamin will not go down there with you! His brother is dead and he is the only child left to me. If any harm were to come to him you would bring my old grey head down to the grave in sorrow.

(*They freeze. The steward crosses the acting area, bearing a card announcing 'some weeks later'. Jacob and his sons come to life again.*)

**Jacob**   My sons, the famine continues to be severe. Go back to Egypt and buy us a little more food.

**Judah**   But the man who is lord of all Egypt warned us solemnly: 'You will not see my face unless your brother is with you.' You

|       | must send Benjamin with us, then we can go down and buy more food. |

**Jacob** Why did you bring this trouble on me by telling this man you had another brother?

**Reuben** He questioned us closely about ourselves and our family. He asked us, 'Is your father alive? Do you have another brother?' We simply answered his questions.

**Judah** Send the boy with me, father, and we will go at once. I myself will guarantee his safety. If I do not bring him back I will bear the blame for the rest of my life. As it is, we are simply wasting time. We could have gone and returned twice!

**Jacob** If it must be, Judah, then do this: take the man some gifts from our land, a little balm and some honey, spices and myrrh; some pistachio nuts and almonds. Take double the amount of silver with you, for you must return the silver that was put back in your sacks. And may God Almighty grant you mercy that the man will let Simeon and Benjamin return with you. As for me, if I am bereaved, I am bereaved.

*(Appropriate action. The brothers, now with Benjamin, set off for Egypt. The steward meets them, then goes to speak to Joseph.)*

**Steward** The men from Canaan have returned to buy more food, O master.

**Joseph** (*Looking across at the group*) I see they have brought their young brother with them. Now, take them to my house, prepare a banquet for them. They are to eat with me at noon.

**Steward** It shall be done.


*(Joseph exits. The steward ushers the group of brothers forward. They are very anxious and suspicious.)*

**Steward** Come, enter my master's house.

**Reuben** What is happening, Judah?

**Judah** Surely he brings us here because of the silver in our sacks. He wants to attack us and overpower us, and steal our slaves and donkeys.

**101**

**Reuben**  (*To the steward*) Good steward of your master, lord of all Egypt. Plead our cause. We came here the first time to buy food. But when we stopped on our way home we found our silver had been returned in our sacks. We don't know how this happened. So we have brought it back. And additional silver to buy more food.

**Steward**  It is all right. Do not be afraid. Your God, the God of your father, must have given you the treasure in your sacks. The grain was paid for. I received your silver. And, look, your brother Simeon is here to join you.

(*Simeon enters, escorted by the guard. Appropriate action. Then Joseph enters and speaks in a more conciliatory tone.*)

**Joseph**  How is your aged father? Is he still living?

**Judah**  He is still alive and well, O great lord of Egypt.

**Joseph**  Is this your youngest brother? (*indicating Benjamin*)

**Reuben**  Yes, sir. This is he.

**Joseph**  God be gracious to you, my child.

(*To the steward, aside*) Steward, serve them their food. Be generous. Give them food and drink from my table. And see that the youngest gets five times as much as anyone else.

**Steward**  It shall be so, master.

(*To the brothers*) Come, a feast is prepared for you.

(*The steward and the brothers exit. The steward returns and addresses Joseph in a conspiratorial manner.*)

**Steward**  Your orders have been carried out, master. The men's sacks have been filled with as much grain as they can carry and we have put their silver back in each sack.

**Joseph**  And my silver cup?

**Steward**  That has been placed in the mouth of the sack of the youngest, as you said. They are now on their way back to their land.

(*The brothers reappear and set off for Canaan.*)

**Joseph**     Go after them. When you catch them up, say to them: 'Why have you repaid good with evil? You have stolen my master's cup.'

**Steward**    I go at once, my lord.

*(Appropriate action. Then, in the centre of the acting area . . .)*

**Steward**    You men, wait. I have a message for you from my lord in Egypt. I must ask you why you have repaid good with evil, by stealing my master's cup?

**Reuben**     *(Aggrieved)* This is not so.

**Simeon**     Why do you say such things?

**Judah**      We even brought back to you the silver we found in our sacks.

**Reuben**     So why should we now steal from your master?

**Judah**      If any of us has stolen from your master, he will willingly be put to death and the rest of us will become your slaves!

**Steward**    Very well. Let it be thus: whoever is found to have my master's silver cup, he will become my master's slave. The rest of you will be free from blame.

**Reuben**     Open your sacks, brothers, and let them be searched.

*(Appropriate action.)*

**Benjamin**   What is this in my sack?

**Judah**      Oh no! It is the silver cup!

**Reuben**     How can this be?

**Simeon**     Now great trouble comes upon this family!

*(They all return to Egypt and confront Joseph.)*

**Judah**      Great lord of Egypt, have mercy on us.

**Simeon**     Spare the life of this our brother, Benjamin, as in your goodness you spared mine.

**Joseph**     *(Mock anger)* What is this you have done? Did you think you could get away with it? Do you not realise I have the power of divination?

**Reuben**     What can we say?

**103**

| | |
|---|---|
| **Judah** | How can we prove that we are innocent of this thing? |
| **Simeon** | We are now in your hands. We are your slaves. |
| **Joseph** | Only the one who was found to have the cup will become my slave. The rest of you are free to return to your father. |
| **Judah** | Please, my lord, let your servant speak a word. Do not be angry with your servant. You will remember, sir, that my father has already lost one son, Joseph by name, surely torn to pieces by wild animals. If you take this one from him too and harm comes to him, death will be the only end to my father's misery. His life is closely bound up with the boy's life. If we return without him, our father will surely die. Sir, I have guaranteed to my father that the boy will return safely. So, please, my lord, let me your servant remain here as your slave and let the boy return with his brothers. |
| **Joseph** | Everyone leave this room, except these men. Immediately! |
| **Steward** | Our master is deeply distressed. Come, let us leave him to deal with these men on his own. |
| | (*He and the guard exit.*) |
| **Joseph** | (*His attitude suddenly changing*) Look at me, brothers, do you not see? I am Joseph. Joseph, your brother. So tell me again, is my father still living? |

(*The brothers react accordingly.*)

| | |
|---|---|
| **Reuben** | It is . . . Joseph? |
| **Judah** | God protect us! |
| **Simeon** | Joseph! |
| **Benjamin** | Joseph? Is he not dead many years? |
| **Joseph** | Come close, my brothers. Look. I am your brother, Joseph. Do not be distressed. And do not be angry with yourselves for what you did to me. It was to save many lives that God sent me here ahead of you. For two years there has been famine, and five more years to come – but God sent me ahead of you, to preserve for himself a remnant and to save your lives. It was not you who sent me here, but God. You meant to harm me, but God intended it for good. |

**104**

**Benjamin**  Is this really my brother Joseph?

**Joseph**  Yes. It is really I, Joseph, who is speaking to you. Now hurry back to our father and tell him that God has made me lord over all Egypt. Then come down to me, all of you; bring my father with you; and you shall live here, close to me, in the region of Goshen, you and your wives and your children and your grandchildren. And I will provide for you. We shall be together, one family, the children of Israel.

(*They all embrace one another.*)

# Farmer Jack

## (*Harvest*)

### Introduction

This is a pantomime version of the parable of the sower. All the acting is mimed. It is intended that the actors should really go 'over the top' in exaggerated, extravagant and enthusiastic performances! Lizzy and Andy were the actual names of two of the original performers of this sketch: obviously these can be changed appropriately if your performers are known to the audience.

### Bible base
*Matthew 13. 1–9, 18–23*

### Cast
Narrators 1 and 2
Jack (farmer/preacher)
Lizzy Corn
Andy Corn
Mummy Corn
Pop Corn
the Bird
Wicked Weed
Sun

*At the start of the play the two Narrators stand on opposite corners of an empty stage.*

**Narrator 1**     This is the tale of farmer Jack.

*(Enter Jack with a heavy sack on his back: appropriate mime.)*

**Narrator 2**     Who lives in a shack.

**Narrator 1**     One day at the crack. . . .

**Narrator 2**     . . . of dawn, Jack . . .

| | |
|---|---|
| Narrator 1 | . . . leaves his shack . . . |
| Narrator 2 | . . . with a heavy sack . . . |
| Narrator 1 | . . . upon his back. |
| Narrator 2 | And down the track . . . |
| Narrator 1 | . . . at the back . . . |
| Narrator 2 | . . . of his shack . . . |
| Narrator 1 | . . . past the haystack . . . |
| Narrator 2 | . . . goes Jack . . . |
| Narrator 1 | . . . with his sack . . .

(*getting in quickly before Narrator 2 can say the next line*) . . . on his back. |
| Narrator 2 | The sack is full of corn . . . |
| Narrator 1 | (*Aside to the audience*)  Rather like this sketch! |
| Narrator 2 | . . . which farmer Jack is going to plant in his fields. He scatters the seed far and wide. Let's find out what happens to four of those little seeds of corn. |

(*Exit Jack, scattering seed. The four seeds enter, line up at the back of the stage. As they are introduced, they step forward and curtsy or bow appropriately, then return to their place.*)

| | |
|---|---|
| Narrator 1 | There's Lizzy Corn. |
| Narrator 2 | And there's Andy Corn. |
| Narrator 1 | There's Mummy Corn. |
| Narrator 2 | And Pop Corn. |
| Narrator 1 | When Farmer Jack threw him out of the sack, poor old Pop Corn went whizzing through the air and landed with a thump, on . . . |

(*Pop Corn mimes appropriately, lands on his bottom, gets up painfully and rubs his bottom.*)

| | |
|---|---|
| Narrator 2 | (*A little prudishly*) . . . the path. |
| Narrator 1 | 'This is not the sort of soil I had in mind,' he thought to himself, looking around. 'A bit hard. More like concrete than John Innes number 2.' |

*(Pop Corn mimes appropriately: stamps his feet, jumps up and down, etc.)*

> 'No, there's no way I can get in here,' he thought. 'Ah well, I'll just sit here, enjoy the sunshine and watch the world go by.'

*(Pop Corn puts up a deckchair, takes off his shirt, relaxes in the deckchair, sunbathing.)*

**Narrator 2** *(Menacingly)* Suddenly, a big, black, ugly-looking bird came flying by, looking for something for dinner.

*(Enter the Bird, miming appropriately.)*

**Narrator 1** *(In a matter-of-fact way)* McDonalds was closed.

**Narrator 2** *(With increasing drama in the voice)* Seeing Pop Corn sitting there on the path, the big bird swooped down, grabbed the poor defenceless seed, and . . .

**Narrator 1** . . . and that, children, was the end of him.

*(Exit Bird and Pop Corn, with appropriate mime.)*

**Narrator 2** Easy pickings there on the path.

**Narrator 1** He didn't stand a chance.

**Narrator 2** Poor little seed.

**Narrator 1** *(Encouraging audience participation)* Aaah!

**Narrator 2** Meanwhile, back at the farm, Andy Corn had flown through the air in a graceful arc, and landed . . .

*(Andy Corn does a graceful, ballerina-style movement out to the front of the stage. He then walks around like someone walking on pebbles without shoes on.)*

**Narrator 1** . . . on some stony ground.

**Narrator 2** 'Well, stone me!' he thought to himself. 'This is more like Brighton Beach than fertile farm-land.' However, with a great deal of effort, he just managed to *squeeze* *(exaggerating this word)* himself between the stones.

**Narrator 1** He was only a little thing.

*(This line is amusing if Andy Corn is on the large side!)*

*(Andy Corn squeezes himself downwards on to the floor and curls up tight. He then gradually unwinds in the best 'Music and Movement' tradition!)*

| | |
|---|---|
| **Narrator 2** | And he soon began to grow. |
| **Narrator 1** | He grew up and up. |
| **Narrator 2** | Higher and higher and higher. |
| **Narrator 1** | And before long he had grown into a fine, handsome-looking plant. |

(*Andy Corn looks round, pleased with himself.*)

| | |
|---|---|
| **Narrator 2** | Next morning he tuned into the BBC weather forecast. |

(*Andy Corn gets out a transistor radio, tunes it and puts it to his ear.*)

| | |
|---|---|
| **Narrator 1** | (*BBC voice*) Today will be overcast and cloudy, heavy showers and rather cool. |
| **Narrator 2** | And so, of course, the sun came out and shone all day. |

(*Enter the Sun: actor carrying a sun on a pole. The Sun stands behind Andy Corn. Andy Corn wipes his brow and mimes appropriately to the following narration.*)

| | |
|---|---|
| **Narrator 1** | It got hotter and hotter. |
| **Narrator 2** | And hotter and hotter. |
| **Narrator 1** | The poor plant started to wilt. |
| **Narrator 2** | Desperately he tried to push his roots further into the shallow soil to find some more moisture. But all he could find were stones getting in his way. It was no good. |
| **Narrator 1** | He just wilted and wilted. And by the end of the day, our fine young plant was just a dried-up, crumpled heap of smelly compost. |
| **Narrator 2** | And that, children, was the end of him. |

(*Farmer drags him off. Exit the Sun.*)

| | |
|---|---|
| **Narrator 1** | Shallow soil, stony ground, hot sun. |
| **Narrator 2** | He didn't stand a chance. |
| **Narrator 1** | Poor little seed. |
| **Narrator 2** | (*Encouraging audience participation*) Aaah! |

**109**

| | |
|---|---|
| **Narrator 1** | Meanwhile, back at the farm, Mummy Corn had bounced off the path, rolled over the stony ground and nestled into a nice, comfortable plot of warm, soggy soil. |

(*Mummy Corn mimes appropriately.*)

| | |
|---|---|
| **Narrator 2** | 'I like it here,' she said to herself. |
| **Narrator 1** | And her roots grew down. |
| **Narrator 2** | And her shoots grew up. |
| **Narrator 1** | And she became a beautiful plant. |
| **Narrator 2** | And everyone said: |
| **Whole cast** | (*On or off-stage, chanting in unison*) |
| | Didn't she do well! |
| **Narrator 1** | But, unknown to Mummy Corn, there started to grow beside her . . . |
| **Narrator 2** | . . . Wicked Weed! |

(*Enter Wicked Weed, suitably dressed like the traditional nasty villain.*)

| | |
|---|---|
| **Narrator 1** | (*Encouraging audience participation*) Hiss! |

(*Wicked Weed creeps up menacingly behind Mummy Corn. The entire cast and narrators join in shouting: 'Look out, behind you!' Mummy Corn responds, 'Where?' Then, 'Behind you!' 'Where?' continues in true pantomime fashion, with Wicked Weed always avoiding Mummy Corn's line of vision. Again the audience should be encouraged to join in.*)

| | |
|---|---|
| **Narrator 2** | But it was too late to warn her. Wicked Weed was strong and powerful, and he choked poor Mummy Corn, until all the life went out of her . . . |

(*Appropriate macabre mime!*)

| | |
|---|---|
| **Narrator 1** | And that, children, was the end of her. |

(*Exit Weed; farmer drags off Mummy Corn.*)

| | |
|---|---|
| **Narrator 2** | Started well, but choked by weed. |
| **Narrator 1** | She didn't stand a chance. |
| **Narrator 2** | Poor little seed. |
| **Narrator 1** | (*With audience*) Aaah! |

**Narrator 2**     (*Brightly*) But, children, the story, though sad so far, does have a happy ending. For listen to the tale of Lizzy Corn.

(*Lizzy Corn steps forward, hands raised in greeting, loud applause and cheers from off-stage, which she cuts after a few seconds.*)

**Narrator 1**     (*Energetically*) Lizzy Corn flew out of the farmer's hand, bounced off the path, did a double somersault over the stony ground, two handsprings and a forward roll over the weeds, and landed feet first on . . .

(*Lizzy Corn looks in horror at the narrator!*)

(*To Lizzy Corn*) . . . all right, you can miss that bit out. And landed feet first in some really good, clean, rich, fertile soil.

(*She walks forward and crouches down, then mimes growing.*)

**Narrator 2**     Soft, moist, no stones, no weeds, good soil, just waiting for a good seed to grow in it.

**Narrator 1**     And her roots grew down.

**Narrator 2**     And her shoots grew up.

**Narrator 1**     And she became a beautiful plant.

**Narrator 2**     And because there was good soil there, with no stones to stunt her growth, and no weeds to choke her life, she produced much fruit.

(*Lizzy Corn takes out an apple and a banana and holds them out at arm's length.*)

**Narrator 1**     And that, children, is the end of the story.

(*Cast reassemble in line at back of stage and take a bow. When applause – if any! – has died down, Narrator 2 continues.*)

**Narrator 2**     (*Talking to Narrator 1*) Well, what was all that about?

(*Jack, now a preacher, steps forward with a Bible in one hand. The four 'seeds' gather round him and listen.*)

**Narrator 1**     Well, Jesus said that it's rather like that whenever the Word of God is preached. Some people will be like the hard soil of the path. The Word is snatched away before it has had a chance to take root.

**111**

*(Pop Corn turns away from preacher, adopts an uninterested pose, takes out a paperback and reads it.)*

> Others are like the shallow, stony ground. They seem interested in God's Word, but give up when things get difficult.

*(The Sun actor passes by and jeers at the seeds listening to the preacher. Andy Corn looks embarrassed, steps away, and stands with his back to the preacher.)*

> Others are like the soil full of weeds. They get so tied up with the cares of this life that the Word gets choked and their spiritual life is squeezed out of them.

*(Mummy Corn takes out the Financial Times, studies it, drifts away from the preacher, and takes up a position with her back towards him.)*

> But some, thank God, are like the good soil. They receive the Word of God deep into their hearts and live by it. They produce lives which bring real glory to God.

*(Lizzy Corn takes the Bible from the preacher, they move forward to centre stage, he with his arm around her shoulder, she studying the Bible intently.)*

**Narrator 2**   And that is what it is like *whenever* the Word of God is proclaimed?

**Narrator 1**   Yep.

**Narrator 2**   *(Thoughtfully)* I see. I wonder, then . . . I wonder what sort of soil we have here this morning?

*(All the actors on the stage and the narrators turn and look pointedly at the audience, and freeze.)*

# Not a lot of people know that

## (*Harvest*)

## Introduction

This dialogue is intended as a contribution to a harvest service. It is assumed that there is a harvest display from which the various items required can be taken.

## Bible base

*Genesis 1. 9–11, 26–31; Genesis 8. 22; Psalms 104, 111, 146, 147; Matthew 6. 25–34*

## Cast

Reader

Know-all

*The dialogue and action all take place in front of the display of harvest produce. If the Know-all is unable to memorise all the lines an alternative is for him or her to carry a large encyclopaedia from which all the information can be read. The Know-all should have a characteristically irritating tone of voice. The Reader should be initially tolerant of the interruptions, but should then get increasingly annoyed as they continue. At the start of the sketch the Reader takes up position as if to read the lesson. The Know-all wanders on during the opening reading and examines the harvest display.*

**Reader**    Our reading this morning is a selection of verses from the Bible on the theme of God's provision of all our material needs in his perfect creation.

(*Reads*) 'Then God said, let the land produce vegetation: seed-bearing plants and trees on the land that bear fruit with seed in it, according to their various kinds. And it was so. The land produced vegetation: plants bearing seed according to their kinds and trees bearing fruit with seeds in it according to their kinds. And God saw that it was . . .'

*(While this is being read, the Know-all selects an apple from the display, examines it with interest, and carries it to the Reader, interrupting him or her by thrusting the apple under their nose.)*

**Know-all**  Did you know . . . that an apple seed contains precisely the right balance of nutrients necessary for the healthy growth of a sapling and furthermore the cells of the seed contain all the genetic information required to determine precisely the shape, size, fruit, leaves and other characteristics of the fully grown apple tree?

**Reader**  Is that a fact?

**Know-all**  Yes. Not a lot of people know that.

*(Wandering back to the display to replace the apple)* Isn't nature wonderful!

**Reader**  *(Continuing to read)*

'So God created man in his own image. In the image of God he created him. Male and female he created them. God blessed them and said to them, be fruitful and increase in number. Fill the earth and subdue it. Rule over the fish of the sea and the birds of the air and over every living creature that moves on the ground. Then God said, I give you every seed-bearing plant on the face of the whole earth and every tree that has fruit with seed in it. They will be yours for food. God saw all that he had made and it was very . . .'

*(This time the Know-all returns with a jar of honey which is thrust under the nose of the Reader.)*

**Know-all**  Did you know . . . that the honey-bee builds its honeycomb in a pattern of tessellating hexagons? And, furthermore, the hexagon, having six sides, is the largest regular polygon for which this is possible, thus ensuring maximum space for the minimum amount of material?

**Reader**  Is that a fact?

**114**

**Know-all**  Yes. Not a lot of people know that.

*(Wandering back to the display to return the honey)* Isn't nature wonderful!

**Reader**  *(Continuing to read)*

'The Lord said in his heart, as long as the earth endures, seed-time and harvest, cold and heat, summer and winter, day and night, will never cease. Great are the works of the Lord. Glorious and majestic are his deeds. He has caused his wonders to be remembered. The Lord is gracious and compassionate. He provides food for those who fear him. He remembers his covenant for ever . . .'

*(This time the Know-all returns with a plant which is thrust under the nose of the Reader.)*

**Know-all**  Did you know . . . that in the Middle East seeds of some plants have been discovered that are over a thousand years old, and yet they are found to be still viable, so that merely with the addition of water and warmth they are still capable of springing into life?

**Reader**  Is that a fact?

**Know-all**  Yes. Not a lot of people know that.

*(Wandering back to the display to return the plant)* Isn't nature wonderful!

**Reader**  *(Continuing to read)*

'The Lord set the earth on its foundations. It can never be moved. He made springs pour water into the ravines, it flows between the mountains. They give water to all the beasts of the field. The wild donkeys quench their thirst. The birds of the air nest by the waters. They sing among the branches. He makes grass grow for the cattle, and plants for man to cultivate, bringing forth food from the earth, wine that gladdens the heart of man, oil to make his face shine, and bread that sustains his heart. How many are your works, O Lord! In wisdom you made them all. The earth is full . . .'

**115**

*(This time the Know-all returns with a loaf of bread which is thrust under the nose of the Reader.)*

**Know-all**  Did you know . . . that a loaf of bread made from wholemeal flour, using all the nutrients contained in the whole grains of wheat, contains, amongst other things, protein essential for the maintenance and growth of body tissues, carbohydrates essential for energy, thiamine essential for sound nerves, niacin essential for healthy skin, calcium and phosphorus essential for strong bones and teeth, iron essential for healthy blood, and dietary fibre essential for a healthy digestive system?

**Reader**  Is that a fact?

**Know-all**  Yes. Not a lot of people know that.

*(Wandering back to the display to return the loaf)* Isn't nature wonderful!

**Reader**  *(Continuing to read)*

'Therefore I tell you, do not worry about your life, what you will eat or drink; or about your body, what you will wear. Is not life more important than food and the body more important than clothes? See how the lilies of the field grow. They do not labour or spin. Yet I tell you that not even Solomon in all his splendour was dressed like one of these. If that is how God clothes the grass of the field, which . . .'

*(This time the Know-all returns with a flower which is thrust under the nose of the Reader.)*

**Know-all**  Did you know that the seeds in many flowers, like sunflowers, daisies and asters, are arranged in perfect logarithmic spirals, and, furthermore, that the number of clockwise spirals and the number of anticlockwise spirals are always successive terms of the mathematical progression known as the Fibonacci series, and, furthermore, that the ratio of these two numbers approximates to the golden section?

**Reader**  Is that a fact?

**Know-all**  Yes. Not a lot of people know that.

*(Beginning to wander back to the display)* Isn't nature wonderful!

**116**

**Reader**     (*Calling the Know-all back*)  Excuse me one minute.

(*Somewhat sharply*) Did *you* know that there are some people in this world who are so short-sighted that they can look at the intricate wonders of what you call 'nature', with all its patterns and laws, its symmetries and varieties, and fail to recognise in it all the handiwork of a good and loving Creator?

**Know-all**   (*A little sheepishly*)  Is that a fact?

**Reader**     Yes! (*Forcefully*) And not a lot of people know that!

(*The Know-all wanders back to the display to replace the flower.*)

**Reader**     (*Continuing to read*)

'Sing to the Lord with thanksgiving. Make music to our God on the harp. He covers the sky with clouds; he supplies the earth with rain and makes grass grow on the hills. He provides food for the cattle and for the young ravens when they call. The Lord delights in those who fear him, who put their hope in his unfailing love. Blessed is he whose hope is in the Lord his God, the maker of heaven and earth, the sea and everything in them – the Lord, who remains faithful for ever. Praise the Lord . . .'

(*During this reading the Know-all looks thoughtfully at the display, then suddenly grabs an armful of produce and runs across to the Reader, again interrupting the reading.*)

**Know-all**   (*Excitedly*)  Excuse me, did you know that . . .

**Reader**     Excuse *me*! But I'm trying to read the Word of God to these people.

**Know-all**   I'm sorry. But I just wanted to say, isn't *God* wonderful!

**Reader**     (*Turning to the Know-all, so that they are face to face, very close to each other*)  Is that a fact?

**Know-all**   Yes. And, furthermore . . .

(*They turn their heads towards the audience, pause, then speak.*)

**Together**   Not a lot of people know that!

**117**

# Tug of war

## (*Alternative Hallowe'en*)

## Introduction

Hallowe'en, of course, exists because it is the day before All Hallows or All Saints Day, the day when the Christian church remembers all the saints who have gone before us. This is an opportunity therefore to celebrate the good things that have been done in the name and in the power of the Lord Jesus Christ. Unfortunately this spot in the Christian calendar has been taken over by the world and exploited by commercial interests, in much the same way as Christmas and now Easter have been. In fact, at its worst, Hallowe'en has now become a celebration of all things nasty and evil. It is encouraging therefore that Christians are at last beginning to respond to the world's distortion of Hallowe'en and are seeking ways of making an alternative, positive statement in support of goodness, beauty and truth. This sketch aims to make clear that a fascination with evil and all the unpleasant things associated with Hallowe'en is not just a harmless bit of fun, but is part of the ongoing battle between God's kingdom of light and the forces of darkness. Clearly some thought needs to be given to the appropriateness of this sketch for various audiences. It is highly suitable, for example, for performance to adults and teenagers, but may not be so appropriate without some modification for performance to an audience containing younger children.

## Bible base

*Exodus 20. 2–3; Matthew 6. 33; Ephesians 5. 8–9; 1 John 1. 5–7;*
*2 Corinthians 6. 14; Matthew 19. 21; Philippians 4. 8; 1 Peter 2. 9;*
*1 Timothy 1. 15*

## Cast

Three actors are required: A, B and C.
A represents God and the Kingdom of Heaven;
B represents Satan and the kingdom of darkness;
C is a representative of the human race.

*There are two screens, one either side of the stage. A is hidden behind the one representing the Kingdom of Heaven. A strong light shines out from behind this screen. B is hidden behind the other screen, representing the kingdom of darkness. A and B deliver their lines from behind the screens, so there is no need for memorising them. They should be amplified, if possible. There are two thick ropes, one each trailing from behind each screen across the stage, meeting approximately in the middle. As the sketch unfolds, A and B have to pull on these ropes creating a tug of war with C in the middle. Throughout the sketch C must react appropriately to the words coming from behind the screens. C enters, stumbles over the two ropes, picks up the end of each in turn and gives a little tug, intrigued . . ..*

A     (*Strong and with authority*) I am the Lord your God. You shall have no other gods before me.

    (*A pulls the rope taut.*)

B     (*Mocking*) How terribly old-fashioned.

A     Seek first the Kingdom of God and his righteousness.

B     Boring!

(*C starts to get pulled towards A.*)

A     Live as a child of the light.

B     Darkness is more fun.

A     For the fruit of the light consists in all goodness . . .

B     Boring.

A     Righteousness . . .

B     Boring, boring, boring.

A     And truth.

B     (*Laughs scornfully*) Oy, you!

(*B's rope is suddenly pulled taut, jerking C back away from A.*)

    What about a little bit of fun? Come on, come over to the darkness.

A     God is light.

B     Just a little stroll in my direction. No harm in that.

(*C now starts to get pulled towards B.*)

A    Walk in the light as he is in the light.

B    Don't listen to all that rot. Follow the crowd.

A    Follow me.

B    Come on, come and dabble a bit over here. Evil is so much more interesting.

A    What fellowship can light have with darkness?

(*C is quite close to B's screen now.*)

B    Just have a little look in this pit. Now isn't that . . . fasc . . . in . . . at . . . ing.

(*Now the tug of war begins in earnest. C is yanked to and fro between A and B during the following sequence. It must be a real battle. A and B should sound as though they are struggling to pull C their way, because they actually are!*)

A    Whatever is true . . .

B    Whatever is false!

A    Whatever is noble . . .

B    Whatever is evil!

A    Whatever is right . . .

B    Whatever is wrong!

A    Whatever is pure . . .

B    Whatever is filthy!

A    Whatever is lovely . . .

B    Whatever is nasty!

A    Whatever is admirable . . .

B    Whatever is worthless!

A    If something is excellent . . .

B    If something is trash!

A    If something is praiseworthy . . .

B    If something is the lowest common denominator of all the ghastly, empty, self-indulgent rubbish that human beings can get entangled with . . .

**A & B** Think about such things!

**A**      I have called you out of darkness . . .

**B**      Come on, don't pretend you're not interested. It's Halloween . . .

**A**      . . . out of darkness into my wonderful light!

**B**      It's only a harmless bit of fun.

(*C now gets pulled towards B; A appears to be losing the battle.*)

We've got black magic and evil spells, video nasties, witches and ghouls, horror comics and horoscopes, Ouija boards, vampire movies, blood-curdling stories of murder, rape, violence, and every conceivable way of exploiting all the nasty and unpleasant side of your human nature. Come on, enjoy yourself!

**A**      Here is . . . (*really struggling to keep hold now*) . . . a trustworthy saying . . .

**B**      Stop worrying. Come closer. Closer, closer.

**A**      This is something really worth holding on to . . .

(*There is a loud drumbeat off-stage and C loses hold of A's rope and sprawls on the ground in the direction of B. C is still holding B's rope, which is pulled taut.*)

**C**      (*Shouting desperately*) God help me!

**A**      Christ Jesus came into the world to save sinners!

**C**      Save me!

(*C looks frantically towards A's screen. After a few moments, A steps out from behind the screen, with his back towards the audience. He reaches out with great effort towards C, who reaches up towards A's outstretched hand. Eventually A is able to grab C's hand. With a supreme effort he pulls C up and free from B's rope. As B's rope is released, B screams loudly in defeat, there is a second loud drumbeat, A moves into an upright position with arms outstretched, suggesting the crucifixion, and C moves into a kneeling position at A's feet. They hold this position for a while. Then A turns and, taking C's hand, leads C off to behind the screen.*)

# Saints alive!

## (All Saints Day)

written by Derek Haylock, Amanda Johnson and Steve Utley,
based on material developed by Norwich Youth for Christ

## Introduction

This piece is based on the principle that instead of celebrating evil and
nasty things at the end of October we can have just as much (and health-
ier) enjoyment celebrating goodness, beauty and truth. It aims to help the
audience to appreciate that 'saints' are not just dead people who lived a
long time ago or pictures in a stained glass window. All those who love
and follow the Lord Jesus, who offer their lives for his service in any way,
are saints. From this idea the piece leads into a celebration of all the good
things that Christians have done and are doing for the sake of Jesus. It is
designed to involve a good number of children as well as three adults. The
examples of 'saints' used in the piece should be adapted to suit local circumstances.

## Bible base

*Romans 1. 7: 'To all . . . who are loved by God and called to be saints.'*

## Cast

Leader

Person A

Person B

about eight children depicting various 'saints'

*The leader is introduced as someone who is going to talk to us about saints. He or
she takes their place on the stage as though about to give a long and probably rather
boring talk. Persons A and B are in the audience, A fairly central and near the
front, B towards the back.*

| | |
|---|---|
| **Leader** | November the first is called All Saints Day. So I'm going to talk to you about some famous saints. When you see a picture of a saint in a church, like in a stained-glass window, you can always recognise them because they have a halo around their head. This shows that they were especially holy people. Saint Christopher, for example. He's one of the most well-known saints. |

*(Person A yawns audibly. The Leader looks displeased.)*

|  | |
|---|---|
| | Saint Christopher is, of course, the patron saint of travellers. Lots of people like to have a little Saint Christopher badge with them when they go on a long journey. |
| **Person A** | *(Under their breath)* I don't believe this . . . |

*(Person A gets up and starts to leave rather obviously. The Leader notices but carries on to begin with.)*

| | |
|---|---|
| **Leader** | I've got a nice little silver Saint Christopher here, that was given to me by . . .. |

*(Person A is now walking down the aisle, shaking their head in some disbelief.)*

| | |
|---|---|
| | Excuse me! Where are you going? |
| **Person A** | *(Stopping, looking a little sheepish)* Who me? Sorry, I'm just leaving . . . |
| **Leader** | *(Forcefully)* But I'm trying to give a talk about saints. |
| **Person A** | So I noticed. |
| | *(Not wanting to make a fuss)* Sorry, but do you mind if I just go now? |
| **Leader** | Well, I don't know. It seems very rude to me. Perhaps you're not interested in All Saints Day? |
| **Person A** | *(Hesitating to get involved)* Well, to tell you the truth I thought it was a bit . . . boring, really. I mean! Saint Christopher, patron saint of travellers! |
| | *(Getting more confident)* It's not exactly inspiring stuff, is it? Next thing you'll be telling us about Saint George and the dragon . . .. |

**123**

| | |
|---|---|
| **Leader** | Well, er, actually . . . (*backing off a little*) |
| **Person A** | Well, if you are going to talk about saints you might start with someone a bit more interesting. There's millions to choose from. |
| **Leader** | Millions? But I've got a book called Legends of the Famous Saints and there's only twelve in that. |
| **Person A** | (*Gradually getting involved*) But some of the less famous ones are more interesting. |
| **Leader** | Like who? |
| **Person A** | Well . . . (*struggling a bit*) |
| **Leader** | Come on then . . . |
| **Person A** | Well, how about . . . Saint . . . Fursey! |
| | (*Bursts out the name as though just making it up!*) |
| **Leader** | Who? |
| **Person A** | (*Going up to the front and gently edging the Leader to one side*) |
| | Yes, Saint Fursey. Look, I'll tell everyone about Saint Fursey, while you just stand over there and see if you can get some inspiration. Right. Here we go. Saint Fursey. Well, I tell you, he was a saint and a half! Not one of your common or garden saints. OK, so not many people have heard of him. But quite a character was Fursey. He was a member of this monastic order in Ireland in the seventh century. |
| **Leader** | He was a monk? |
| | (*With irony*) That sounds really interesting! |
| **Person A** | Yes, but he wasn't one of your average all-singing, chanting, praying monks, locked away behind the walls of the monastery. Fursey and his mates were so excited about the good news of Jesus that they decided that God wanted them to take it all round the world. But Ireland, you see, is an island. So they set to and built themselves a boat. No ordinary boat though. It was made of pigskin – they had lots of pigs in Ireland – but it had no sails, no oars, not even a rudder. |

| | |
|---|---|
| **Leader** | So he wasn't much of a boat-builder, this Fursey-bloke? |
| **Person A** | Well, I must admit it does sound like a pretty hopeless boat – but Fursey and his crew believed that if they prayed and trusted God, then he would take them to some foreign shore where they could start to spread the good news of Jesus. |
| **Leader** | So when did they set off on this crazy journey? |
| **Person A** | It was around six-thirty. |
| **Leader** | What, six-thirty in the morning? |
| **Person A** | No, dimwit, in the year 630. Without any maps, without a compass, without any navigation charts, and without any means of steering their crazy little boat, they launched into the sea, with no idea where they might finish up. |
| **Leader** | At the bottom of the sea, I should think! |
| **Person A** | But God was in control. And finally, after drifting for some weeks, they landed on the foreign shore they had prayed for. It was Cornwall. And from there they set about preaching the good news of Jesus right across southern England. Loads of people became Christians. Eventually Fursey found himself in Norwich. He was welcomed by King Sigebert, king of the East Angles, who was keen to learn about Christianity – and Fursey set up his mission headquarters at Burgh Castle near Great Yarmouth. So, you see, thanks to Fursey and his crazy boat trip, people in East Anglia came to hear about Jesus. |
| | (*Turning to Leader*) Well, have you thought of any interesting saints yet? |
| **Leader** | Er-um . . . |
| **Person B** | (*Calling out*) I have! |
| **Leader** | Who said that? |
| **Person B** | Me! |
| | (*Standing and starting to move*) I've thought of one. |

**125**

| | |
|---|---|
| **Leader** | Who? |
| **Person B** | Saint Jackie! |
| **Leader** | Who? |
| **Person B** | (*Now arriving at the front*) |
| | Saint Jackie – Jackie Pullinger. Now she's an interesting saint. When she was a still a teenager she became convinced that God was calling her to serve him overseas somewhere. So she raised enough money to go to Hong Kong. There she worked, for a long time on her own, in the name of Jesus, helping drug addicts, prostitutes and other people in need. Since then, the work has grown so much that she now has teams of Christians set up throughout Hong Kong, working with the homeless and the outcasts from society. They've set up drug rehabilitation centres and seen people rescued from their addiction by the power of the Lord Jesus Christ. |
| **Person A** | She sounds like a real saint! |
| **Leader** | Hang on a bit. Let me get this straight. Don't you have to be dead to be a saint? |
| **Person A** | Nope. |
| **Leader** | And you don't have to be in a stained-glass window with a halo round your head to be a saint? |
| **Person B** | (*To A*) I think (s)he's getting it! |
| **Leader** | So who is a saint then? |
| **Person A** | Anyone who loves the Lord Jesus and believes that he died for them. |
| **Person B** | Anyone who commits themselves to serving him. |
| **Leader** | You mean, any real Christian is a saint! |
| **A & B** | (S)he's got it! |
| **Leader** | Saints Alive! |
| | (*To A*) So, you're a saint! |
| **Person A** | Yep. |

**126**

| | |
|---|---|
| **Leader** | (*To B*) And you're a saint! |
| **Person B** | And so are you! |

(*A and B now point to various known Christians in the audience.*)

| | |
|---|---|
| **Person A** | And, look, there's Saint Tracey. |
| **Person B** | And there's Saint Tony. |

(*And so on . . .* )

| | |
|---|---|
| **Person A** | (*To Leader*) Want some more? |
| **Leader** | Yes, please, this is getting interesting! |
| **Person A** | OK, then, let's meet some saints, some living, some dead. Let's see, who have we got? |

(*Now eight or so young people, representing various 'saints' and dressed appropriately, come quickly on to the stage, one at a time, in rapid succession, and form a group around the Leader. The examples given below can be replaced by others as appropriate to local circumstances or interests.*)

**Child 1**   I'm Hudson Taylor. I'm a saint because I loved the Lord Jesus. And because I loved him I wanted to serve him. So I took the good news of Jesus to millions of people living in inland China.

**Child 2**   I'm Mother Julian of Norwich. I'm a saint because I loved the Lord Jesus. And because I loved him I wanted to serve him. So I wrote about the wonder and greatness of God's love so that others would be led to worship him.

**Child 3**   I'm Lord Shaftesbury. I'm a saint because I loved the Lord Jesus. And because I loved him I wanted to serve him. So I helped to abolish slavery and worked with the poor and homeless.

**Child 4**   (*Leaping appropriately on to the stage*)

I'm the triple-jump world-record holder, Jonathan Edwards. I'm a saint because I love the Lord Jesus. And because I love him I want to serve him. So, as I travel round the world to international athletics events, I take every opportunity I can to tell people about Jesus.

| Child 5 | I'm Mother Teresa. I'm a saint because I love the Lord Jesus. And because I love him I want to serve him. So I've spent my life working with the dying and the outcasts in the Indian city of Calcutta. |
|---|---|
| Child 6 | I'm M.A.F. Pilot Graham Starling. I'm a saint because I love the Lord Jesus. And because I love him I want to serve him. So I fly across the wildest parts of Africa transporting Christian doctors, nurses and other workers, and sometimes carrying desperately-ill patients to hospital. |
| Child 7 | I'm Amy Carmichael. I'm a saint because I loved the Lord Jesus. And because I loved him I wanted to serve him. So I set up a Christian orphanage in South India to look after abandoned children and to show them God's love. |
| Child 8 | I'm not Cliff Richard – but I wish I was! Cliff's a saint because he loves the Lord Jesus. And because he loves him he wants to serve him. So he tells people about God's love through his music, and he gives a lot of his time to help the international relief work of TEAR Fund. |
| Leader | Wow! What a lot of saints, and what a lot of good things done in the name of Jesus! Why don't we celebrate what these saints have done! |
| Person A | Great! Let's celebrate all the good things that Christians today and throughout the ages have done in the name of Jesus! |
| Person B | Let's have a procession of saints! |
| Leader | And some music, please . . .. |

(*As appropriate to local circumstances, they now organise a procession around the church or hall. The audience or congregation sing, for example, 'Oh, when the saints come marching in . . .' The children dressed as saints are joined by others carrying percussion instruments. Go for a real party atmosphere. Have party-poppers and balloons planted amongst likely members of the audience to release as the procession passes.*)

| | |
|---|---|
| **Leader** | (*When the procession is ready to go and the music is about to start*) |
| | OK! Let's celebrate . . . all those who are loved by God, and called to be . . . |
| **Leader, A & B** | . . . saints! |

(*Music! Action!*)

# The National Society

The National Society (Church of England) for Promoting Religious Education supports everyone involved in Christian education – teachers, school governors, students, parents, clergy, parish and diocesan education teams – with the resources of its RE centres, courses, conferences and archives.

Founded in 1811, the Society was chiefly responsible for setting up the nationwide network of Church schools in England and Wales, and still helps them with legal and administrative advice for headteachers and governors. It was also a pioneer in teacher education through the Church colleges. The Society now provides resources for those responsible for RE and worship in any school, lecturers and students in colleges, and clergy and lay people in parish education. It publishes a wide range of books and booklets and the magazine *Together with Children* for leaders of children's work.

The National Society is a voluntary body that works in partnership with the Church of England General Synod Board of Education and the Division for Education of the Church of Wales. An Anglican society, it also operates ecumenically, and helps to promote inter-faith education and dialogue through its RE centres.

For a free resources catalogue and details of individual, corporate and associate membership contact:

> The Promotions Officer
> The National Society
> Church House
> Great Smith Street
> London SW1P 3NZ
> Telephone: 0171-222 1672
> Fax: 0171-233 2592

# Plays on the Word
Derek Haylock

A collection of eighteen sketches that are ideal for family services, school assemblies, youth clubs and church drama groups. Topics range from a TV newscast report of the Crucifixion and Resurrection to an illustration of the Christian response to environmental issues and a challenge to Christmas-only churchgoers. In each sketch a serious message about the gospel is conveyed clearly through the humour and entertainment.

# Sketches from Scripture
Derek Haylock

Twelve short, fast-moving drama sketches, designed to be performed with minimum rehearsal. They include The Prodigal Daughter (a new twist to the familiar story), A Grave Business (the story of the raising of Lazarus) and The Least of These (focusing on the needs of children worldwide).